SWAZILAND
JUMBO TOURIST GUIDE

5th Edition . 1995

written by
HAZEL A. HUSSEY

A Travel Guide for Tourists and Visitors
to the Kingdom of Swaziland

Published by and printed for Jumbo Publications (Pty) Ltd.
P.O. Box A225, Swazi Plaza, Mbabane, Kingdom of Swaziland.
Tel: (+268) 46416, 44522, Fax: (+268) 42485

I.S.B.N. No: 0-620-18892-8

PINDAR — SCARBOROUGH U.K.

THE SWAZILAND JUMBO TOURIST GUIDE

ACKNOWLEDGEMENTS

The publishers would like to acknowledge and thank the following persons and organizations for their valuable support and contributions.

All of the companies and individuals who have supported this guide in the form of advertising.

His Royal Highness, the Honourable Minister Prince Phinda
Minister of Broadcasting, Information and Tourism for writing the foreword to this guide.

To Neville Pritchard who designed the cover and gave invaluable assistance with the overall design. To David Adelsburg, Edmund Nzima. To Jo Kentgens and Sun International, Pauline Woodall, Marc and Liz Ward, Aleta and Peter Armstrong. To Ted and Liz Reilly for their invaluable contributions to this edition and to Darren Raw for his ideas and enthusiasm. To Albert Nxumalo, Len Morison and Royal Swazi Airways, Horst Saylor, June Thomas and Ruth Buck. To Dr Busa Xaba and The Swaziland Sugar Association, Solly Nkabinde and the Shell Petroleum Company. To Pat Forsyth-Thompson, To the Staff of the Reference Library, Mbabane, To Barclays, Standard Chartered, Stanbic, Meridien and Swaziland Development Bank for their ongoing support. To Tibiyo Insurance Brokers and Swaziland Insurance Brokers for their advice and encouragement.

To Steve Hall for his selection of photographs, to Hayley Hussey for her input in taking and choosing suitable slides and to Rod de Vletter for his pictorial contribution. To Andy Duff and the team at Graphco for their attention to detail and professional advice. To Zodwa Dlamini for all her hard work and tremendous support with this edition. Cartography by courtesy of the Surveyor General's Office, Mbabane.

No part of this publication may be reproduced, stored in a retrieval system, or transmitted in any form or by any means, electronic, mechanical, photocopying, recording or otherwise, without the prior written permission of the Copyright owner.

Details and prices contained in this Guide were correct at time of compilation and the publishers cannot accept responsibility for inaccuracies due to subsequent change.

© Copyright: Jumbo Publications (Pty) Ltd.

Layout, design typesetting	:	Jumbo Publications, Mbabane
Colour separations Make up	:	Graphco Processing.
Cover Design	:	Pritchard Productions.
Printed by	:	Colorpress.

Southern Africa

FOREWORD BY

His Royal Highness, the Honourable Minister
Prince Phinda,
Minister of Broadcasting, Information and Tourism

It is a great pleasure for me to write the foreword to this 5th Edition of the Swaziland Jumbo Tourist Guide. The past year has seen many changes in the Southern African region, most importantly, the successful elections in South Africa and the emergence of a strong regional tourism awareness which of course includes the Kingdom of Swaziland. We also welcome the democratic election in neighbouring Mozambique, so many of our visitors travel to the Kingdom from this country whose borders are so close to our own.

Swaziland is an historical land giving the visitor the opportunity to see the oldest iron ore mine in the world at Ngwenya which dates back to 41,000 B.C. The workings and caves are of great archealogical interest, as they confirm the presence of man and industry long before modern day progress.

The Swazi people are happy, peaceful and friendly and wish to share their Kingdom with caring people from all over the world. We want you to enjoy our magnificent, undulating scenery, our old and rich traditions, our top class hotels and conference facilities, our varied sporting activities, diverse Nature Reserves and the fabric of this Kingdom which makes it unique in the region.

PRINCE PHINDA
MINISTER FOR BROADCASTING, INFORMATION AND TOURISM

Here you can experience the charm and elegance of bygone times in a place where ancient legends blend with the luxuries of modern-day Africa. Whether you're here for a quiet, relaxing break or a holiday filled with activity and entertainment, the Royal Swazi Sun Valley has it all - a magnificent range of sport and leisure options, luxury accommodation and superb restaurants. Of course, we also promise the level of service excellence you would expect from a Sun International Hotel and Casino Resort. The Royal Swazi Sun, Ezulwini Sun and Lugogo Sun. Three Sun International resorts in one spectacular setting.

To experience the magic of Africa, book your stay in the Royal Swazi Sun Valley. Call Sun International Central Reservations:

JHB (011) 780 - 7800

DBN (031) 304 - 9237

REDISCOVER THE ELEGANCE OF THE ROYAL SWAZI SUN VALLEY. WHERE THE MAGIC OF AFRICA LIVES ON.

Royal SWAZI SUN VALLEY

A SUN INTERNATIONAL RESORT

View of the Ezulwini Valley from the Malagwane Hill

CONTENTS

Page

CHAPTER 1 Introduction, Background History, Traditions, Rituals, General Information to assist prior to your visit to Swaziland. Helpful information after you arrive in the Kingdom. 9

CHAPTER 2 The journey from Oshoek/Ngwenya to Mbabane, Handicraft Centres, Mbabane the Capital, Mbabane Hotels, Mbabane Market, The Swazi Plaza, The Mall. 49

CHAPTER 3 The journey through the Ezulwini Valley, Health and Beauty Spa, Sun International Hotels, Independent Hotels, Resorts, Restaurants, Handicraft Centres, Mlilwane Wildlife Sanctuary. 71

CHAPTER 4 The Royal Area of Lobamba, The Houses of Parliament, The National Museum, Lozitha Palace, The Malkerns Valley, Handicraft Centres, The Hub of the Nation - Manzini. 93

CHAPTER 5 The South and West of Swaziland, The Journey from Mahamba to Manzini, The Nhlangano Sun Hotel, The Grand Valley. The Journey from Nerston/Sandlane to Bhunya, Usutu Pulp Mill, Mhlambanyati to Mbabane, Hotels, Resorts. The journey from Bhunya to Malkerns. The journey from Malkerns to Mankayane and Nhlangano. 109

CHAPTER 6	The South East and East of Swaziland. The journey from Lavumisa to Manzini, Hotels, Mkhaya Nature Reserve. The Journey from Lavumisa to Nhlangano.	117
CHAPTER 7	The North East of Swaziland. The journey from Bordergate/Mananga to Manzini. Mlawula Nature Reserve. Hlane National Park. Circular Drive of North East Swaziland Lomahasha entry to Swaziland from Mozambique.	129
CHAPTER 8	The North West of Swaziland. The journey from Jeppes Reef/Matsamo to Mbabane. Protea Piggs Peak Hotel and Casino. Phophoyane Nature Reserve. Havelock. Malolotja Nature Reserve. Hawana Park, Ngwenya Iron Ore Mine.	141
CHAPTER 9	Areas of interest surrounding Swaziland. Mozambique. Kruger National Park. Zululand Parks, The Eastern Transvaal.	155
BIBLIOGRAPHY		161
GLOSSARY	of Hotels, Resorts (Places to stay) Nature and Game Reserves, Restaurants & Places to eat, Shopping for tourists, Transportation.	162
LIST OF ADVERTISERS		170

WEBSTER'S

Hippo - "Amazing!!!"
Cat - "What is?"
Owl - "Their selection of videos, of course!"
Snake - "AND their stationery"
Leopard - "AND their books"
Snail - "AND their service!"
Baby Owl - "AND their educational toys"

WEBSTER'S
Mbabane   Nhlangano
Manzini   Siteki
Piggs Peak

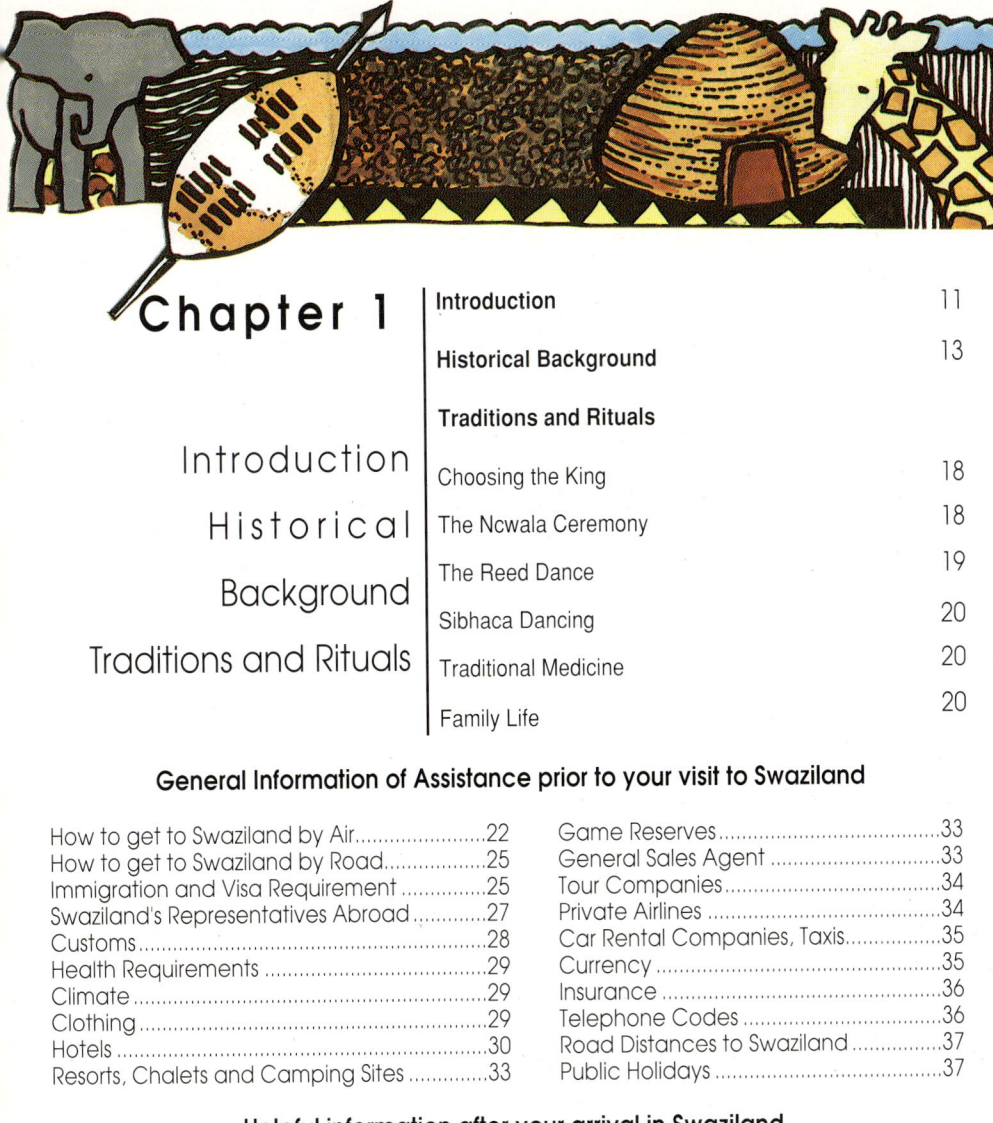

Chapter 1

Introduction
Historical
Background
Traditions and Rituals

Introduction	11
Historical Background	13
Traditions and Rituals	
Choosing the King	18
The Ncwala Ceremony	18
The Reed Dance	19
Sibhaca Dancing	20
Traditional Medicine	20
Family Life	20

General Information of Assistance prior to your visit to Swaziland

How to get to Swaziland by Air	22
How to get to Swaziland by Road	25
Immigration and Visa Requirement	25
Swaziland's Representatives Abroad	27
Customs	28
Health Requirements	29
Climate	29
Clothing	29
Hotels	30
Resorts, Chalets and Camping Sites	33
Game Reserves	33
General Sales Agent	33
Tour Companies	34
Private Airlines	34
Car Rental Companies, Taxis	35
Currency	35
Insurance	36
Telephone Codes	36
Road Distances to Swaziland	37
Public Holidays	37

Helpful information after your arrival in Swaziland

Language	38
Banking	38
Commercial Hours	41
Petrol Hours	41
Garages	41
Churches	42
Hospitals	42
Police	42
Fire	42
Post Offices	41
Service Clubs	44
Assistance Groups	44
Sporting Facilities	44
Foreign Representatives resident in Swaziland	47

His Majesty King Mswati III, Sovereign Head of the Kingdom of Swaziland. Photo by Steve Hall

INTRODUCTION

This is the Fifth Edition of The Swaziland Jumbo Tourist Guide.

The exciting events in neighbouring South Africa and Mozambique have had a positive impact upon Swaziland which represents a haven of peace and tranquillity in the region. As the sole monarchy in Southern Africa, the Kingdom remains a stable and easily accessible country rich in scenic beauty and traditional values. The anticipated increase in the numbers of tourists who wish to visit this friendly nation has prompted a need for further information upon its origins, people, customs and attractions.

In the past twelve months, the routes from Mozambique to Swaziland have bustled with incoming road traffic. Visitors from this area come to Swaziland to experience the cool climate, the excellent range of hotels, natural and man made attractions and the wide selection of goods in the shops. In addition, greater numbers come from South Africa and the neighbouring states heralding increased movement within the region and a thirst for knowledge of cultural, social and economic differences, A number of hotels, resorts, restaurants and craft workshops have been established or changed hands bringing new ideas, different facilities and a dynamic approach to the Tourist Industry. Both international and regional visitors will appreciate these changes and wish to visit the Kingdom of Swaziland returning again and again.

This publication is a practical guide and does not aspire to be an authority upon the history, geography, politics, tradition or economy of the Kingdom. The reader should consult other publications to derive a deeper understanding of this very colourful and intriguing country.

Swaziland is divided from north to south into four distinct geographical regions. The Highveld, forested with indigenous and exotic trees, endless peaks, rushing waterfalls and cool, crisp, champagne air. The Middleveld drops gently in altitude to fertile valleys

The rich soil of the middleveld of Swaziland

where fruit, crops and vegetables thrive in the balmy climate. The Lowveld, still and hot where the dense bush of the National Parks meet the sugar cane and cotton crops of the Eastern Regions. Finally, the mountainous region of Lubombo, dividing Swaziland from Mozambique and the sea; here the three great rivers, the Umbuluzi, the Usutu and the Ngwavuma flow out of the Kingdom towards the Indian Ocean. Within a very small area, Swaziland contains diverse geographic and geological phenomena which can be explored without the need to travel great distances.

Bound to the north, south and west by the Republic of South Africa and to the east by Mozambique, Swaziland is well placed as a tourist destination. International air carriers fly regularly to neighbouring countries and the visitor may continue his journey on Royal Swazi National Airways into Swaziland.

The Kingdom of Swaziland is an independent monarchy fiercely proud of her traditions and heritage. King Mswati III is the executive head of the people of Swaziland and her laws and customs are prescribed through parliament and consultation. It is important for the visitor to know that Swaziland is a sovereign state completely independent from South Africa politically, ideologically, culturally and in practice.

The marriage of two ages within the Kingdom is highly successful. Daily the visitor will see both men and women dressed in the colourful Emahiya acknowledging traditional values.

Swazi men frequently wear animal skins according to their status in Swazi culture and carry knobkerries, spears, battle axes and shields for ceremonial occasions. Swazi customs are conservative; based upon the stability of the extended family and always taking their lead from the traditional practice and ancient example. Yet modern technology is also present in the Kingdom, large industrial companies operate and prosper. This is partly due to the encouragement by the Swaziland Government to attract international investment and to the stable political climate existing within the Kingdom which attracts Western interest and capital.

Located within the four geographical regions are luxury casino hotels, exceptional independent hotels, hideaway resorts, cosy family hotels, self catering chalets and camping sites, wildlife sanctuaries, reserves and parks plus a wealth of walking and climbing trails. Sporting facilities are varied including tennis, wonderful golf courses, squash, bowls, horse riding, swimming, putt putt, fishing and rock climbing.

A variety of crafts indigenous to the Swazi people can be seen in production, ordered and purchased. Breathtaking scenery which nearly overwhelms the visitor in its variety and beauty

His Majesty King Mswati III with H.R.H. Prince Andrew at the 25th Anniversary celebrations.
Photo by Steve Hall

contributes to the theory that Swaziland is the "Switzerland of Africa". The Kingdom is rugged, rolling, remote and unspoilt yet offers visitors the sophistication and comfort of top class hotels, restaurants, casinos and intimate pubs and the beauty of natural resources, wild life and well run National Parks.
The two faces of Swaziland; natural beauty and originality coupled with western style comfort await the visitor to explore, enjoy and experience.

HISTORICAL BACKGROUND

Swaziland is the only Kingdom in Southern Africa. King Hussein's Morocco in North Africa completes the duo of African monarchies. The Kingdom of Swaziland once spread from Lourenco Marques in Maputoland in the East to the Limpopo River which separates modern day Zimbabwe and South Africa. Today, Swaziland covers an area of 17,364 square kilometres (6,704 sq. miles), the size of Wales, Kuwait or Hawaii and negotiations continue,to restore the areas of Kangwane and Ingwavume, which were once part of the Kingdom. In recent months these negotiations have taken a very positive turn as the Swaziland Government discusses its southern border with the KwaZulu representatives.
The Kings of Swaziland date back some considerable time to when the Royal line of Dlamini lived in the vicinity of Delgoa Bay. The Nguni people are recorded as having entered the territory of Swaziland around the year 1600. Under the leadership of Dlamini III, settlement took place in 1750, along the Pongola River where it cuts through the Lubombo Mountains. The land they entered was neither vacant nor sparsely populated, it was teeming with game, rich in natural minerals, a haven for crop raising and cattle rearing. Trade had been transacted from the coast for many years, a powerful state of Shiselwini existed which the leaders of the Swazis sought to absorb or overcome.
Ngwani III who is revered in present day Swazi ritual, established his headquarters at Dwaleni which boasted middle and lowveld climates and grazing areas. Here the competition for prime sites and well watered soil necessitated assimilation and defeat of rival clans. Expansion continued to the west and further north; Ngwane III died and is buried in the hills surmounting the Pongola, the evergreen mountain known as Embilaneni is the last resting place of all Swazi kings.
This was the time of the " Mfecane" when Zulu hegemony threatened the entire sub region. Sobhuza I, grandson of Ngwane III built upon the expansion policies of his grandfather, he colonised the north and west absorbing Sotho, Tsonga and Nguni chiefdoms. He moved north to escape the Zulu threat, establishing his headquarters at Hlatikulu, and then at Ezulwini. Those who went with Sobhuza to Ezulwini are known as " Pure Swazi ", those who were absorbed are known as " Those found ahead " and those people who migrated in order to escape the "Mfecane" are known as " Those who arrived after ". Thus a new Swazi nation was born, Sobhuza colonised the north, assimilated the immigrants fleeing from the Zulu threat and based his centre in the fertile area of Ezulwini, dotted with fortress caves within the Mdvimba mountains. Swaziland originally stretched as far as the Sabie River and Steenkampsberg.
Sobhuza I met Shaka's threat with diplomacy,marrying two of his daughters to the Zulu

Maidens at the annual Umhlanga Dance. Photo by Steve Hall

leader, he outlived Shaka and brought a period of peace and growth to Swaziland culminating in the defeat of the Zulus under Dingane at Hlatikulu in 1836. Before Sobhuza died, he is believed to have had a dream of white people, with hair like cattle tails, carrying a book and money pieces. He advised his people never to harm the white people, to accept the book (the Bible), but to refuse the money which could corrupt.

Sobhuza I must be seen as the founder of pre-colonial Swaziland.
Mswati I the son of Sobhuza 1 was a minor at the time of his father's death. His mother, Thandile ruled as Queen Regent. She was a clever woman, mindful of the need to consolidate the central power of the King and the cohesive support of the people. The Ncwala ceremony has its origins from this period; this sacred annual occasion re-affirms the interdependency of the Nation and the King. Central power lies in agricultural production and this "First Fruits Ceremony" binds the regiments and the King consolidating kinship and loyalty.
In addition, Thandile created the Age Regiments forming a military framework from a network of Royal villages as regimental rallying points who acted as support for the King and as monitors of political activities.
Mswati formed strong diplomatic links with the Boers and the British as a political powerbase against the watchful Zulus. In 1847, Mswati moved the capital to the Hhohho area north of the Komati river distancing himself from his southern enemies. His power gradually enveloped the north and east giving access to ivory trade and cattle. The area between the Pongola, Crocodile and Limpopo rivers formed part of Mswati's domain and in 1863 the Swazis attacked Lourenco Marques where a small garrison of Portuguese soldiers was defeated. The Portuguese power and prestige in the area, always reliant upon political alliances, collapsed and the Swazis were the dominant power in the area for 15 years.
Mswati I died in 1865 having created a cohesive ruling class, followed an aggressive foreign policy and established a sound political base for growth. During his reign the nation became known as "Swaziland" or the land of the people of Mswati.
There followed a period of peace during the Queen Regent's reign prior to the accession of Mbandzeni. The Boers wished to expand to the sea to compete with the British; overtures were made to secure the route through Swaziland to Kosi Bay. These proved unsuccessful;and Swaziland became a pawn between the two powers which culminated in the notorious Concession period. King Mbandzeni tried to secure the continued

independence of Swaziland through a series of grazing, mining and trade concessions which ironically lost the territorial independence of the Nation.
Mbandzeni requested the assistance of Theosophilus Shepstone from Natal who did little to really assist the Swazi people. In desparation, Mbandzeni turned to the British for help but continued to concede large parcels of land to unscrupulous agents, adventurers and opportunists in order to escape the land grabbing of the South African Republic.
By 1889, the land which Mswati I had formed was in tatters, Swazi independence a shell, the nation had become a pawn in the Imperialist game. The Boers sought Swazi minerals, the route to the sea and her pasture land, the British drew political maps suited to her expansionist policies which lost a large area of Swaziland and until 1894 the Kingdom was ruled by a provisional government of Boer, British and Swazi. King Mbanzeni granted a Charter of Self Government to the European settlers who resided or had interests in the Kingdom, this was to deal with their own affairs but always subject to the King's veto. The concessions were offered for a limited period; many have fallen away in recent years allowing the land and rights to revert back to the Crown. By 1894, Swaziland became a protected dependency of the South African Republic under King Bhunya's reign. This monarch, who was considered cruel and callous, was summoned to court for executing a chief, the British Government supported him declaring that " there was not a court competent enough to try a King". Following the confrontation of the two powers in the Anglo Boer War in 1902, Swaziland was placed under British rule which continued to administer the Kingdom as a Protectorate until 1968 when the Nation gained independence.
The Queen Regent, Gwamile became the custodian of Royal power until the accession of Sobhuza II when he was 21 years. Queen Gwamile recognised the importance of books as the foundation of growth to the Nation. Schools were established and young Sobhuza was sent to a Mission school in South Africa from where he returned as "Ngwenyama" to tackle the concession problems.
Throughout his long reign, King Sobhuza devoted himself to regaining the land of the Kingdom now in the hands of private individuals or companies. A fund was established contributed to by Swazis which was used to repurchase land. By 1968, the year of Independence, over half of the land conceded had been restored to the Swazi Nation. Now no foreigner may purchase land without the approval of the Land Control board. King Sobhuza's reign must be seen as a long period of stablity during which the economy expanded and foreign investment flowed in. The balance of investment changed, favouring the South African investor, British capital still dominates the banking and agro-industrialist sector but there is a growing reliance upon South African capital partly from membership of the Customs Union and as part of the Rand Monetary Area. Swaziland's traditional rulers acquired a material base in the capitalist system through the purchase of shares in the major foreign companies and the establishment of farms and businesses in the private sector. This was effected in tandem with the control of the non-capitalist sector through the communal land tenure system.
In 1978, the Parliament of Swaziland as it operates today was established. Parliament is elected to the two chambers of the House. His Majesty retains full executive and legislative powers but in consensus with his Council of State, his cabinet, his members of parliament and his people. In 1993, a more democratic government was established with full national franchise and representation in line

with United Nations and World Bank's criteia.
In 1982, King Sobhuza died having steered his country and people through the 2nd World War where the people of Swaziland contributed their valour and their lives, past Independence, towards economic and political growth in a period noted for its stability and progress.
Following the death of King Sobhuza II, the Queen Regent, Dzcliwe assumed the regency. As in previous accession times, this period was marked by unrest and jockeying for power. The Liqoqo or Supreme Council of State came into conflict with the Prime Minister, a confused time ensued until the arrival of the young heir to the throne, Prince Makhosetive who had been educated at Sherborne School, Dorset, England. In 1983, a new Parliament was elected and in 1986, King Mswati III was crowned at a great celebration attended by many Heads of State.

H.M. King Mswati III with King Goodwill at Somhlolo Stadium.
Photo by Steve Hall

King Mswati III is now ruler of the Kingdom of Swaziland, in 1993 he celebrated his 25th birthday and the 25th anniversary of the Independence of Swaziland. In October 1989, His Majesty visited the United Nations and was the youngest ruler to address that body. Swaziland continues to follow a traditional, conservative path interlinking Swazi customs with modern, Western initiative and technology. In order to assist the underprivileged, King Mswati established a body known as " The King's Trust " which is funded from the profits accrued from Annual Music Concerts performed at the Somhlolo Stadium. Under the King's leadership and guidance, great strides have recently been made with road and bridge re-construction and general improvements in the infrastructure to facilitate the rapid development of the industrial and tourism base of Swaziland. Major construction of new projects have taken place in 1994, most notably the arterial road between Matsapha and Manzini.
His Majesty, King Mswati III rules as executive Head of State and as spiritual leader of his people. The King or "Ngwenyama" (The Lion) as he is officially known is imbued with spiritual and sacred qualities, he is guardian of his subjects and their mouth piece, fulfilling a dual role of leader and custodian of the country and people of Swaziland.
The Kingdom of Swaziland today is composed of an homogenous population who share language, culture and loyalty to their King and country. There are no tribal conflicts, the Kingdom is stable, orderly and at peace with her neighbours. Perhaps, Swaziland's greatest asset is her people, who are invariably happy, friendly, courteous and willing to assist visitors to their Kingdom. A visit to Swaziland is for the free in spirit to enjoy the cosmopolitan society, the freedom of movement and the beauty of the land. The visitor is safe in Swaziland and free to go where he chooses and with whom, providing, of course, he respects the culture and traditions of these very courteous people and obeys their laws.

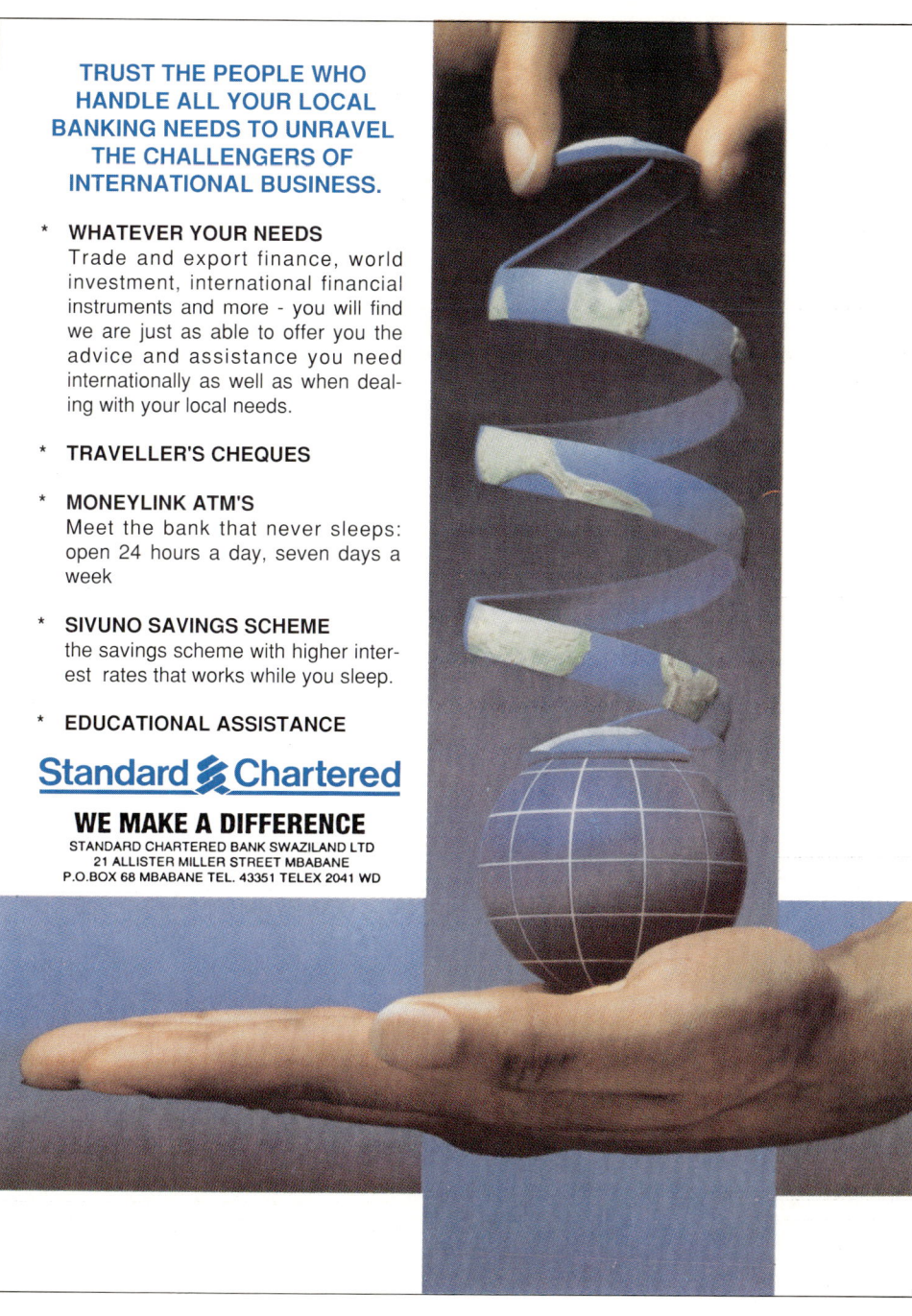

TRUST THE PEOPLE WHO HANDLE ALL YOUR LOCAL BANKING NEEDS TO UNRAVEL THE CHALLENGERS OF INTERNATIONAL BUSINESS.

* **WHATEVER YOUR NEEDS**
  Trade and export finance, world investment, international financial instruments and more - you will find we are just as able to offer you the advice and assistance you need internationally as well as when dealing with your local needs.

* **TRAVELLER'S CHEQUES**

* **MONEYLINK ATM'S**
  Meet the bank that never sleeps: open 24 hours a day, seven days a week

* **SIVUNO SAVINGS SCHEME**
  the savings scheme with higher interest rates that works while you sleep.

* **EDUCATIONAL ASSISTANCE**

Standard Chartered

WE MAKE A DIFFERENCE
STANDARD CHARTERED BANK SWAZILAND LTD
21 ALLISTER MILLER STREET MBABANE
P.O.BOX 68 MBABANE TEL. 43351 TELEX 2041 WD

TRADITIONS AND RITUALS: CHOOSING THE KING

The successor to the throne is chosen in relation to the status of his mother. A Queen Mother is selected because of her high rank, however, the Queen Mother will be chosen by the Royal Council after the King's death, she will be from an unrelated family. The Royal family line, the Dlamini's, never intermarry; the King is always a Dlamini, the Queen Mother is never a Dlamini. The Queen Mother may have only one son, as a king is not to be followed by blood brothers. He is "Nkosi Dlamini" and is expected to unify his position by choosing wives from all sectors of the community.

The balance of power lies between the King and the Queen Mother; the "Ngwenyama" represents the hardness as expressed in thunder, the Queen Mother or "Ndlovukazi" (The Elephant) the softness as in water. They assist and advise each other in many activities, each complementing the other.

The Royal Council plays a key role in the selection of the successor to the throne. He must be single and if still a minor, the Queen Mother to the late King automatically assumes responsibility of Regent until the prince is crowned "Ngwenyama". The present Queen Mother, Queen Ntombi ruled as Queen Regent until King Mswati III was crowned in April 1986.

THE NCWALA CEREMONY

The Ncwala or first fruit ceremony is the most sacred of all the Swazi ceremonies in which the King plays a dominant part. When there is no King, the Ncwala remains in abeyance. The Ncwala is usually held in December or January upon a date chosen carefully by Swazi astrologers in conjunction with the position of the sun relating to the phases of the

Umhlanga Dance Princesses dance before their Majesties. Photo by Steve Hall

moon. The ritual begins with the journey of the Bemanti or "the people of the water" to the ocean off Mozambique where they collect the foam from the waves. The return to the Royal Cattle Kraal commences in the celebration of the "Little Incwala", which precedes the appearance of the full moon. Following the little Ncwala, youths journey in groups to every corner of the Kingdom to collect the sacred branches of the "Lusekwane" shrub which is a species of acacia. Tradition dictates that the leaves of the shrub will wilt in the hands of any youth who has been intimate with a married woman or has impregnated a young maiden. The lusekwane is taken to the Royal byre to build a small enclosure.

Upon the third day a bull is ritually slaughtered by the groups of youths. This promotes solidarity among the young men and a spirit of valour which is essential in fostering national unity, loyalty and discipline.

The boys who are too young to take part in the lusekwane gathering, stack the imbondvo tree branches around the enclosure. The fourth day of the Ncwala is the culmination of this sacred ritual, when the King, in full ceremonial dress, joins his warriors, in the traditional Ncwala dance. The King then enters a special hut within the sacred enclosure and after further rituals, he eats the fruits of the new season. Upon the appearance of the King to his people, the Swazi nation can eat the first fruits with the blessing of their ancestors. The final burning of the King's bedding and household items follows, thus cleansing everything in readiness for the new year. Traditionally it is forbidden to eat the young fruits and vegetables of the season until His Majesty has first tasted them.

Photographs may not be taken of certain parts of the ceremony and permission should be sought in writing from the Government Information Service, P.O. Box 338, Mbabane.

THE UMHLANGA OR REED DANCE

The Reed Dance or Umhlanga takes place in late August or early September each year. It is a dance which attracts maidens from every area of the Kingdom and provides the occasion for them to honour and pay homage to the Queen Mother (Ndlovukazi).

Most of the maidens who take part are in their teens, although there are some younger ones who participate. During the first week the young maidens gather reeds from specially selected areas, some of the older girls travel a long distance, leaving the young ones to choose reeds close to their homes. The day of the Reed dance begins with bathing and grooming prior to appearing before the King and Queen

Swazi girl in pensive mood. Photo by Steve Hall

Mother. The girls wear short beaded skirts decorated with fringes and buttons; together with anklets, bracelets and necklaces and colourful sashes. Each sash has appendages of different coloured wool streamers; these denote whether or not the maiden is betrothed. The Royal Family Princesses wear red feathers in their hair and lead the maidens to perform for their Majesties. Each group has its own particular dance steps and song which marks their respect for the Monarch and his mother. Many of the girls carry torches to indicate that they had cut the reeds at night. The Reed Dance attracts young maidens and young men from across the Kingdom and fosters the unity of the clans which characterises modern Swaziland as devoid of tribal differences. Photographs may be taken at the Reed Dance.

SIBHACA DANCING

Sibhaca dancing is vigorous and performed by teams of men throughout the Kingdom. Many schools encourage Sibhaca dancing among the young boys who form their own teams and perform at special occasions. Big Game Parks have their own Sibhaca dance teams at each of their reserves and the Royal Swazi Sun have two teams of dancers who will show their prowess when requested. Tourists should check at the Government Tourist Office as to where and when Sibhaca Dancing is to be performed.

TRADITIONAL MEDICINE

Traditional healers in Swaziland are regarded as physicians, prophets, priests, herbalists and diviners which places a great responsibility upon them. Approximately 80% of the Swazi Nation consult them and there are both male and female traditional healers.

The "Inyanga" inherits his skills from his grandfather and father. His profession is dominated by men and the "Inyanga" holds a senior place in Swazi society. His main function is divination which may be effected by throwing the bones.

After several throws when the bones fall into different patterns, the "Inyanga" will scrutinise them and then spell out a clear message in lyrical siSwati.

The "Sangoma" is a traditional healer who has been "called" to the profession. Generally practised by women, the "Sangoma" is consulted to alleviate physical and mental problems, to attend various ceremonies and to act as a counsellor. When divining, the "Sangoma" relies traditionally upon spirit possession. Both the "Inyanga" and the "Sangoma" are herbalists and their profession is encouraged by the Swaziland Government. A special school is maintained at Siteki and visits to the school can be pre-arranged.

FAMILY LIFE

Originally a clan system existed in Swaziland which was structured as follows:
Nkosi Dlamini: Close blood ties and high status - aristocracy
Bearer of Kings: The class who have provided Queen Mothers.
Clans with own areas and hereditary chiefs.
Clans from whom officials are selected for rituals and administration.
Through marriage these clans have intermingled but there is still a class system which

regulates marriage. Within the aristocracy, the first wife is never the main wife, status is very important and a second wife who has a higher pedigree will take precedence.

A preferential marriage is arranged by the parents which bestows a higher status upon the union forming a permanent bond between the families. The bridegrooms's family provide the desired number of cattle "lobola" in keeping with the bride's family background and the marriage ceremony may take several days before the bride is finally annointed to indicate that the marriage has taken place.

In a private marriage, when there is no public ceremony, the girls parents may oppose the marriage, or the girl has no family or funds to provide the public ceremony.

The arrival of a child in a Swazi home is a source of great joy to all the members of the family. However, the rights of fatherhood are acquired through the "lobola" or dowry. If no cattle have been given the child remains with the mother's family. Swazi families are usually

Smiling Umhlanga dancer. Photo by Steve Hall

large operating in the extended tradition. The child will be taught to share both the fruits and problems of life with the other family members. Discipline and a share of family responsibility is ingrained in the child from an early age. The father is the head of the homestead, his authority is respected and obeyed. Boys will be taught by male members of the family and assume male roles and skills, similarly, girls will learn from their mothers and female relations.

Boys enter regiments in which they will train with others of similar age, growing with the same group throughout life. The regiment's members are expected to support each other and close friendships are formed across clan boundaries. Only when the young man reaches mature warrior status does he consider courtship, as his previous responsibilites involved participation in national projects and festivals.

Grandparents teach the young to respect their parents. Old age is treated with great respect within the Swazi Culture as the social, political and religious roles gain importance within the family unit. Grandparents can also act as a counter balance between parents and their children lending their wisdom and counsel in times of strife.

INFORMATION OF ASSISTANCE PRIOR TO YOUR VISIT TO SWAZILAND.

HOW TO GET TO SWAZILAND BY AIR

Matsapha Airport is the National airport located 8 kms from Manzini. The National Airline **ROYAL SWAZI AIRWAYS** flies regularly from Kenya, Mozambique, South Africa, Tanzania, Uganda, Zambia and Zimbabwe into the Kingdom of Swaziland. The National airline operates 10 flights a week from and to Johannesburg and 4 flights from and to Cape Town which interconnect with flights from Europe, the Americas, Australisia and the Far East. In addition Comair fly from Johannesburg and AirLink from Durban to Swaziland.

The following airlines fly regularly into Matsapha Airport:

AIRLINK	- DURBAN	- TUES, WEDS, FRI, SUN.
AIR ZIMBABWE	- HARARE	- TUESDAY
COMAIR	- JOHANNESBURG	- TUES, WEDS, SAT.
L.A.M.	- MAPUTO	- FRI, SUN
LESOTHO AIRWAYS	- MASERU	- TUESDAY

SWAZILAND - PAST AND PRESENT

Two essential reference books for visitors to Swaziland

IN THE TRACKS OF THE SWAZI PAST

A historical tour of pre-colonial Swaziland which brings to life the culture and vibrancy of one of the oldest societies in Africa.

SWAZILAND

A magnificent full colour visual tribute to Swaziland. The book captures the beautiful scenery, culture and traditions of a proud and peaceful nation.

AVAILABLE FROM ALL BOOKSHOPS IN SWAZILAND

Published by:
  Macmillan Boleswa Publishers
  P O Box 1235, Manzini, Swaziland
  Tel: (268) 84533/84834/84535   Fax: (268) 85247

Macmillan Boleswa

Through our wide range of products we serve commerce, construction, forestry, farming and transport.
Through our resources we serve education, culture and numerous charities.
Oh yes, and through our pumps we serve petrol.
Engen. Serving the needs of the Nation.

With us you are Number One

HOW TO GET TO SWAZILAND BY ROAD

Swaziland has 12 entrance posts, located around the Kingdom with the busiest being, Ngwenya/Oshoek in the West, Lavumisa/Golela in the South East and Mahamba in the South. Border times are as follows and are open 365 days a Year.

BULEMBU/JOSEFSDAL	08h00-16h00
GEGE/BOTHASHOOP	08h00-16h00
LAVUMISA/GOLELA	07h00-22h00
LOMAHASHA/NAMAACHA	07h00-16h45
LUNDZI/WAVERLEY	08h00-16h00
MAHAMBA	07h00-22h00
MANANGA/BORDERGATE	08h00-18h00
MATSAMO/JEPPE'S REEF	07h00-18h00
NGWENYA/OSHOEK	07h00-22h00
SALITHIE/ONVERWACHT	08h00-16h00
SANDLANE/NERSTON	08h00-18h00
SICUNUSA/HOUDKOP	08h00-16h00

All of the major roads leading into Swaziland are tarred and others are regularly maintained gravel roads. The road between Mbabane and Mhlambanyatsi has been tarred as has that between Siteki and Big Bend. Currrently being upgraded is the road beween Matsapha and Manzini and, the route between Mlawula and Bordergate. Motorists must remember to observe the general speed limit of 80km per hour and 60km per hour in built up areas. The Royal Swaziland Police Force are extremely polite but vigilant in the control of excessive speeds on the roads. As Swaziland is a very mountainous country, roads are winding and steep in places, it is wise to observe the speed limit and to assume defensive driving techniques. A road tax of E5.00 is levied upon entry at Border Posts.

VISAS AND IMMIGRATION REQUIREMENTS

All visitors require a valid passport or travel document which must be registered with an immigration officer or police station upon arrival.
The following visitors are **exempt** from visas.
Nationals of Swaziland, **British** subjects being "Citizen of the United Kingdom and Colonies". Nationals of: **Australia, Bahamas, Barbados, Belgium, Botswana, Canada, Cyprus, Denmark, Finland, Gambia, Ghana, Greece, Grenada, Guyana, Iceland, Republic of Ireland, Italy, Jamaica, Kenya, Lesotho, Liechtenstein, Luxembourg, Malawi, Malaysia, Malta, Nauru, Netherlands, New Zealand, Nigeria, Norway, Papua New Guinea, Portugal, Samoa (Western), San Marino, Seychelles, Sierra Leone, Singapore, Solomon Islands, Republic of South Africa, Sweden, Tanzania, Tonga, Trinidad and Tobago, Uganda, The United States of America, Zambia and Zimbabwe.**
Nationals of the **European Community Countries,** (other than British subjects), Austria, **Switzerland** and the **Republic of China** require Visas which may be obtained free of charge at the Swaziland border posts and airport..
Visas are issued by the Chief Immigration Oficer based in Mbabane:

The Chief Immigration Officer, P.O. Box 372, Mbabane, Swaziland. Telephone 42941/2 or from the Swaziland Missions and Consulates stationed abroad. Visitors arriving from or through South Africa may obtain visas from:

The Swaziland High Commission P.O. Box 8030, Johannesburg, 165, Jeppe Street, Tel: (268) 11 299 776/7, Fax: (268) 11 299 763

Visitors wishing to remain in Swaziland for longer than 60 days must apply for a temporary residence permit from the Chief Immigration Officer in Mbabane.

Visitors who need a visa to enter South Africa, should ensure that they have a multiple entry visa before leaving South Africa to enter Swaziland. Swaziland is a separate diplomatic and political entity from South Africa.. Visitors who wish to travel on to Mozambique must also obtain visas from the Mozambique Embassy in Mbabane.
The large border post at Ngwenya has speeded up the entry process and the South African Immigration authorities no longer require foreign Nationals to complete immigration forms on entry or exit.

NEW ROAD

As part of the Lome Convention agreement, Swaziland is constructing a dual carriageway between the city centres of Mbabane and Manzini. This is a major undertaking as it the arterial road and lifeline of the Kingdom upon which all commercial and private traffic travels. The tortuous Malagwane Hill connecting Mbabane with the Ezulwini Valley is to have an additional carriageway carrying heavy traffic away from the holiday leisure area towards Matsapha. There will be some disruption whilst the new carriageways are are being constructed, however, the contractors are making deviations and alternative routes to facilitate smooth traffic flow.

Aerial view of the City of Mbabane

DIPLOMATIC REPRESENTATION
Swaziland's Representatives Abroad

MISSIONS
United Nations: Swaziland's Permanent Mission to the United Nations
866 United Nations Plaza
Suite 420, New York, N.Y. 10017
United States of America   Telex: 620670
Tel: (212) 371-8910   Fax: (212) 754-2755

European Community
Kingdom of Swaziland Mission to the E.E.C.
Rue Joseph II, 71,   5th Floor, (Boite 8)
8-1040 Brussels, Belgium.
Tel: 02/230.00.44, 02/230.01.69
Fax: 02/230.50.89   Telex: 26254

EMBASSIES
United Kingdom
Swaziland High Commission
58 Pont Street, Knightsbridge
London SW1X 0AE   Tel: 071-581-4976/7/8
Fax: 071-589-5332   Telex: 28853 G

Canada
Swaziland High Commission
130 Albert Street
Ottawa, Ontario
KIP 5G4   Canada
Tel: (613) 567-1480   Fax: (613) 567-1058

Denmark
Embassy of the Kingdom of Swaziland
Kastelsvej 19
3rd Floor
DK-2100 Copenhagen, Denmark
Tel: (31) 42 61 11/2/3 Fax: (31) 42 63 00
Telex: 15810 Swazi DK

Kenya
Swaziland High Commission
SIlo Park, 3rd Floor, Mama Ngina Street
P.O. Box 41887, Nairobi, Kenya
Tel: 00254-2-339-231/2/3
Fax: 00254-2-330540   Telex: 22085 Swazi

Korea
Embassy of the Kingdom of Swaziland
Garden Tower Building 1706
98-75 Wooni-dong, Chongro-ku
K.P.O Box 1387
Seoul, Republic of Korea
Tel: 744-0263/4

Mozambique
Embassy of the Kingdom of Swaziland
AV do Zimbabwe 608
P.O. Box 4711
Maputo, Mozambique
Tel: 492451, 491721, 491656
Fax: 492117   Telex: 6353

United States of America
Embassy of the Kingdom of Swaziland
3400 International Drive
Suite 3M, Washington D.C. 20008
Tel: (202)362-6683/4/5
Fax: (202) 244-8059   Telex: SWAZI 64435

HONORARY CONSULATES ABROAD
Greece
Consulate of the Kingdom of Swaziland
88 Drossopoulos Street
Athens 4, Greece

Israel
Consulate of the Kingdom of Swaziland
1 Seadya Gaon Street, Jerusalem 92267, Israel

Japan
Consulate of the Kingdom of Swaziland
1 Kanda Izumi-cho
Chiyonda-Ku, Tokyo 101, Japan

Spain
Consulate of the Kingdom of Swaziland
23, Santa Beatriz De Sila
Magada Honda, Madrid, Spain

Switzerland
Consulate of the Kingdom of Swaziland
CH-8039 Zurich
Talstrasse 58, Switzerland

Taiwan
Consulate of the Kingdom of Swaziland
3rd Floor, 53, Nangking
East Road, Section 2
Taipei, Taiwan, Republic of China

West Germany
Consulate of the Kingdom of Swaziland
D-4 Dusseldorf 1
Worringer Strasse 59
P.O. Box 4209, West Germany

HIGH COMMISSION
Republic of South Africa
Swaziland Trade Mission, 165 Jeppe Street,
The Rand Central Building, Room 915-921, 9th Fl.
P.O. Box 8030, Johannesburg, 2000, R.S.A
Tel: (011) 29 9776/8   Fax: (011) 29 9763
Telex: 484114 SWTMN SA

CUSTOMS

Swaziland belongs to the Common Customs Union together with South Africa, Botswana, Lesotho.

Visitors who live outside of the Customs Union of Southern Africa; that is tourists from Europe, USA, the Far East, Middle East, South America and Australasia should note the following customs regulations. These regulations apply also to visitors from African States.

1. All tourists may bring personal effects for their own comfort and convenience whilst on holiday.
2. Such personal effects include clothing, personal jewellery, cameras, films, sporting and recreational and camping equipment.
3. Duty free allowances include 400 cigarettes, 50 cigars, 250 grams tobacco,
2 litres of wine, 500ml perfume, 250ml toilet water, 1 litre of spirits.

Visitors are requested to make a declaration of their luggage upon arrival, as all goods imported into Swaziland are subject to Custom control. Every Rand's worth of goods declared in an honest declaration means a percentage of duty is awarded to Swaziland from the Customs Union pool.

Visitors who come from the Common Customs Area may bring unlimited amounts of goods for their own personal use. These must be declared but are not subject to duty. Arms and ammunition are prohibited, unless prior permission has been granted by the Firearms Licensing Board, P.O. Box 49, Mbabane.

MBABANE PHARMACY

Allister Miller Street (opp. Standard Bank), MBABANE

PHILANI PHARMACY

Swazi Plaza, MBABANE

For all your medicinal needs while on holiday
Contact the LEADING PHARMACIES

HEALTH REQUIREMENTS

Visitors who eminate from an endemic yellow fever or cholera area should possess valid innoculation certificates upon entry into Swaziland. Swaziland and South Africa are not in an endemic area.

Health regulations do change from time to time, so do check with the Embassies, Trade Missions or Consulates abroad or the Chief Immigration Officer which regulations are in force. Visitors should be aware of the dangers of bilharzia in stagnant water or water close to habitation.

Malaria is endemic in certain parts of the Kingdom and visitors should take prophylactic drugs at least two weeks prior to arrival, during their stay and two weeks after leaving Swaziland. Anti-malaria drugs are readily available from your doctor or pharmacy and additional supplies can be obtained at chemists in Swaziland.

CLIMATE

Swaziland has one of the best climates in the world. Due to the four separate regions and their elevations, the tourist can find a suitably cool or warm climate within the Kingdom.

The seasons are the reverse of the Northern Hemisphere; December is mid Summer and June is mid Winter. Summer rains fall between November and April and some spectacular thunder storms can occur during these months. The Winter months are from June to August when temperatures in the Highveld can be cool to cold at night. Conversely, the Lowveld can be very hot in Summer reaching levels of 40C.

Visitors should note that the Nature reserves are at their best in the Winter months when the vegetation is less dense.

Birdspotting is best experienced in the Summer months when the migratory species have returned home. Each region has its own special climate to attract the visitor and all may be experienced within a single day. Average temperatures at Mbabane are as follows:

SPRING:	September	- October	20C
SUMMER:	November	- March	24C
AUTUMN:	April	- May	20C
WINTER:	June	- August	15C

CLOTHING

The tourist does not need to bring a wardrobe of formal clothes to Swaziland. Dress is generally casual by day and casually smart in the evenings. It is wise to pack a jersey for cool nights. Gentlemen are expected to wear a jacket and tie in the evening at the smart hotels and restaurants and ladies to wear a smart dress, however, this is not necessary at the more casual venues. Safari suits with long or short trousers, slacks, shorts and casual shirts for men by day and slacks, shorts, summer dresses, skirts and blouses for the ladies. Do bring a pair of good walking shoes for morning walks and mountain trails. Pack the essentials and have fun choosing something different whilst on holiday.

HOTELS

Hotels are not graded in the Kingdom of Swaziland. The following are listed in alphabetical order under the area in which they are situated. The suffix "L"."M", "R", AND"VR" indicate Luxury, Medium, Reasonable and Very Reasonable hotel rates. These are only a guide and visitors should check prior to booking as to the facilities and rates of their chosen hotel. Further information about hotels will be found in later chapters.

Big Bend
The New Bend Inn Hotel (VR) P.O. Box 37, Big Bend Tel & Fax: 36112,
Riverside Hotel (R) P.O Box 110,Big Bend Tel: 36012 Fax: 36032

Ezulwini Valley
Ezulwini Sun (M) P.O. Box 123, Ezulwini Tel: 61201,Telex: 2147 WD,Fax:61782
Happy Valley Motel (R) P.O. Box 5, Ezulwini, Tel: 61061/61199, Fax: 61050
Lugogo Sun (M) Private Bag, Ezulwini, Tel: 61101, Telex 2058 WD, Fax: 61111
Mantenga Lodge(R) P.O.Box 68,Ezulwini, Tel & Fax: 61049.
Mgenule's Motel (VR) P.O.Box 711, Mbabane, Tel: 61041/2, Fax: 46465
Royal Swazi Sun (L) Private Bag, Ezulwini Tel: 61001, Telex: 2014 WD & 2275 WD Fax: 61606 & 61128.
Yen Saan Hotel, (R) P.O. Box 771, Mbabane Tel: 61052, Telex: 2247 WD. Fax: 61051

Manzini
The New George Hotel (M) P.O. Box 51, Manzini Tel: 52061/4, Telex: 2071 WD Fax: 52061
The Mozambique Hotel (R) P.O. Box 417, Manzini,Tel: 52489/52586 Fax: 54044
Prince Velebantfu Hotel, (VR) P.O. Box 48, Manzini, Tel: 52663, Fax 46465

Mantenga Lodge in the Ezulwini Valley. Photo by Fotostudio

Mbabane
City Inn (VR) P.O. Box 15, Mbabane Tel: 42406/42034, Fax: 42034
Mountain Inn (M) P.O. Box 223, Mbabane Tel:42781/42799/42773, Telex: 2135 WD Fax: 45393
Swazi Inn (M) P.O. Box 121, Mbabane Tel: 42235/6, Fax: 46465
The Tavern (R) P.O. Box 25, Mbabane Tel: 42361/2, 42454 Telex: 2306 WD, Fax: 40373

Mhlambanyatsi
The Foresters Arms Hotel (M) P.O.Box 14, Mhlambanyati, Tel: 74177/74377, Telex 2050 WD, Fax: 74051

Nhlangano
The Nhlangano Sun (M) Private Bag Nhlangano, Tel: 78211, Telex: 2089 WD, Fax: 78402
The Phoenix Hotel, (VR) P.O. Box 360, Nhlangano, Tel: 78488

Piggs Peak
Protea Pigg's Peak Hotel & Casino (L) P.O.Box 385, Pigg's Peak, Tel: 71104/5, Telex: 2089 WD, Fax: 71382 & 71325
Highlands Inn, (VR) P.O. Box 12, Piggs Peak, Tel: 71144

Siteki
Siteki Hotel (R) P.O.Box 33,Siteki, Tel: 34126

Tshaneni
Impala Arms Hotel (R) P.O. Box 34, Tshaneni, Tel: 31244

The swimming pool and terrace at the Protea Piggs Peak Hotel

RESORTS, CHALETS AND CARAVAN SITES
Ezulwini Valley
Smokey Mountain Village, P.O. Box 21, Ezulwini Tel: ,61291, 61293 Fax: 46465
Timbali Caravan Park, P.O. Box 1, Ezulwini Tel: 61156
Pigg's Peak
Phophonyane Lodge & Nature Reserve P.O. Box 199, Piggs Peak Tel: 71319/71429 Fax: 71319
Mhlambanyatsi
Meikles Mount, Country Estate, P.O. Box 13, Mhlambanyati Tel: 74110
Motshane
Hawana Park, P.O. Box A225, Swazi Plaza, Mbabane, Tel: 44522/46416, Fax: 42485

GAME AND NATURE RESERVES
Hlane Royal National Park, P.O. Box 234, Mbabane Tel: 44541 Fax: 40957
After hours and weekends Tel: 61037 or 61591/2/3, Fax: 61594
Malolotja Nature Reserve, P.O. Box 100, Lobamba Tel: 61179 Fax: 61875
also P.O. Box 1797, Mbabane Tel: 43060
Mkhaya Game Reserve, P.O. Box 234, Mbabane Tel: 44541 Fax: 40957
After hours and weekends 61037 or 61591/2/3 Fax; 61594
Mlawula Nature Reserve, P.O. Box 100, Lobamba Tel: 61179 Fax: 61875
also P.O. Box 312, Simunye. Tel: 38239
Mlilwane Wildlife Sanctuary, P.O. Box 234, Mbabane Tel: 44541 Fax: 40957
After hours and weekends Tel: 61037 or 61591/2/3, Fax: 61594

GENERAL SALES AGENT
Umhlanga Tours & Safaris act as general sales agents for hotels, resorts, camping, fishing and touring plus Nature Reserves within Swaziland and beyond the borders of Swaziland.
They will compile a complete holiday for the tourist.
Umhlanga Tours & Safaris P.O. Box 2197, Mbabane, Tel: 46416/44522, Fax: 42485

The Traditional Mbabane Craft Market. Photo by Fotostudio

White rhino under the tree canopy at Mkhaya Game Reserve

UMHLANGA TOURS (PTY) LTD

Half day and full day tours of the handcrafts,
Big Game Parks and the magnificent
scenery of Swaziland.
Highly personalised tours where every one
is a very special guest.
Call us for our unique 3 - 5 day tours staying at the best hotels
or in the luxury bushcamp of Mkhaya.
CLOSE ENCOUNTERS with the endangered species
an exceptional opportunity for close up photography.
We also tour to the Kruger National Park, Maputo
and to Shakaland.

**at the Tour Desk, Royal Swazi Sun Hotel
for further details: Tel: 44522, 46416.   Fax 42485
P.O. Box 2197, Mbabane, Kingdom of Swaziland**

Luphophlo Dam en route to Usutu Forest. Photo by Fotostudio

TOUR COMPANIES

Eco-Africa Safaris, P.O. Box 199, Pigg's Peak , Tel: 71319/71429, Fax : 71319,
Umhlanga Tours & Safaris, P.O. Box 2197, Mbabane, Tel: 46416/44522, Fax 42485

PRIVATE AIRLINES

Scan Air Charter Ltd. operate small aircraft for tours within the Kingdom, they also fly tourists and business visitors to the surrounding territories and have offices at Matsapha International Airport and at Maputo. Emergency medical cases are flown to hospitals outside of Swaziland in times of crisis.

Operating a fleet of light aircraft seating five or nine persons, this can be an exciting way to see Swaziland's differing geographic regions and the wildlife within her parks.
Scan Air Charter Ltd. Matsapha Airport, P.O. Box 1231, Manzini, Tel: 84474/84331, after hours: 52673, Telex 2350 WD. Fax 86340.
Maputo Tel: 465592 / 465074/82, Fax: 465525.

CAR HIRE

Visitors arriving at Matsapha International Airport may contact either Avis or Hertz/Imperial Car rental who both have desks in the arrivals hall.

Small, medium and large sedan cars are available from both companies and for touring the visitor may prefer to take a minibus. Renting can commence from the airport, your hotel or a private address. Car Rental normally is charged on a day's rental plus a km charge or on an unlimited km basis for longer rentals. Rates include maintenance, oil, basic insurance, maps and lots of assistance from the company's staff. Collision Damage Waiver and Personal Accident Insurance are extra as is fuel.

Both Avis and Hertz/Imperial operate a one-way rental scheme where a drop off charge will be levied for all stations outside of the Kingdom of Swaziland. Reservations can be made from any Avis or Hertz Office worldwide. Naturally, Avis and Hertz charge cards are welcome, as are American Express, Diners Club, Mastercharge/Access and Visa charge cards.

Avis:
Matsapha Airport	Tel:	84928/86226
Depot	Tel:	86350/86222
After hours	Tel:	38623
Telex 3008	Fax:	86227

Hertz/Imperial
Matsapha Airport	Tel:	84393/84862
	Fax:	84396
Mbabane	Tel:	41384
	Fax:	40459

General details and conditions of car rental are as follows:

Driving Licences - Valid, unendorsed
Minimum Age - 23 or 25 years
Deposit - Cash or recognised, indate credit cards

TAXIS AND AIRPORT/HOTEL SHUTTLE BUS

Taxis operate from the Airport to hotels and the main towns. Visitors should be very careful of the condition of the taxi. Approximate costs are: Matsapha Airport to the Ezulwini Valley - E60, to Mbabane - E70, to Manzini - E50. Umhlanga Tours in conjunction with the major hotels in Mbabane and Ezulwini operate a shuttle bus to and from the airport.

CURRENCY AND BANKING

Swaziland's unit of currency is the Lilangeni (plural Emalangeni) which is equivalent to the South African Rand. Both Emalangeni and Rand are acceptable in all hotels, shops and restaurants, however, South African coins are no longer legal currency within the Kingdom. Travellers cheques may be exchanged at banks and hotels and all leading credit cards are acceptable. Remember to change your Emalangeni back into Rand before leaving the Kingdom or keep the small change as a souvenir. Emalangeni are not negotiable outside of Swaziland.

Automatic teller machines are installed by many banks and certain recognised credit cards can be used to supply cash. Many of the commercial banks will transact cash upon the production of recognised credit cards. Stanbic Bank operates closely with Standard Bank of South Africa, their International Trade Centre deals with all aspects of foreign currency transactions in line with world wide computerised banking methods.

TiB
TIBIYO

TIBIYO INSURANCE BROKERS
(PTY) LTD.

INSURANCE BROKERS TO THE SWAZI NATION

☎ **42010**
43541

Embassy House,
Morris Street
P.O. Box A166, Swazi Plaza,
Mbabane
Telex: 2170 WD
Fax: 45035

INSURANCE

It is always prudent to arrange adequate insurance cover prior to travelling. Good travel and medical insurance promotes peace of mind and should be arranged through your broker before leaving for a visit to Swaziland. If you are arriving by road, be sure to check that your car insurance and third party disc are in date and displayed together with your annual road tax licence. In addition, a policy to cover your personal effects while away ensures adequate cover against all contingencies.

It is wise to record the serial numbers of any valuable items you may carry, such as cameras, binoculars, radios, videos, etc.

Medical health schemes and insurance cover the possibility of illness or accident when on holiday. Remember to bring your medical aid membership number with you. You may find that it is necessary to pay for treatment and drugs at time of consultation and then apply for reimbursement from your own scheme.

Leading insurance brokers with worldwide connections operate within Swaziland. They will assist in times of emergency and give advice regarding claim procedures. Keeping a record of policy numbers with you can help to save wasted time and stress when overcoming a crisis.

TELEPHONE CODE

The International code for Swaziland is 268. Certain countries do not have an automatic connection with Swaziland. Callers from U.K. dial 00268. From South Africa 09268. Please check your phone book for the correct code. The advent of cellular phones in South Africa may well spread to Swaziland, but at present telephone services can be slow and difficult in the more remote areas.

FOTORAMA

Colour film development and printing,
Colour slide processing and mounting,
Black & white developing and printing,
Enlargements, in fact most things photographic.

Close personal attention to your requirements

**Shop 8A, Development House, Swazi Plaza, Mbabane
PO Box 761, Mbabane Tel: 44250 Fax: 42485**

ROAD DISTANCES TO THE CAPITAL OF SWAZILAND

Cape Town /Mbabane	1662 km	Lusaka/ Mbabane	1741 kms
Durban/Mbabane	635 Kms	Maputo/Mbabane	236 kms
Gaborone/Mbabane	718 kms	Maseru/Mbabane	736 kms
Harare/Mbabane	1234 kms	Richards Bay/Mbabane	343 kms
Johannesburg/Mbabane	371 kms		

PUBLIC HOLIDAYS

January 1st	New Years Day	22nd July	Public Holiday
Good Friday		August/Sept	Umhlanga Dance
Easter Monday		6th Sept	Independence
19th April	King's Birthday	25th Dec	Christmas Day
25th April	National Flag Day	26th Dec	Boxing Day
Ascension Day		Dec/Jan	Incwala Day

HELPFUL INFORMATION AFTER YOU ARRIVE IN THE KINGDOM

Language
Siswati and English are the two official languages. Most Swazi people in the urban areas speak and understand English very well. English is the medium of instruction in schools, of communication in business and commerce. Parliamentary affairs are discussed in both languages. Two English newspapers are published daily, The Times of Swaziland and The Swazi Observer. The Sunday Times of Swaziland and the Weekend Observer are circulated each week.

Banking
Visitors who arrive at Matsapha Airport may change their travellers cheques at the Swaziland Development and Savings Bank counter in the main Arrivals hall. In general it is wise to travel with a few rand notes which can be used for taxis, etc. There are 5 commercial banks in Swaziland and their hours of business are as itemised below.

BARCLAYS BANK OF SWAZILAND LTD. P.O. BOX 667, MBABANE.
Tel: 42691/7, Telex: 2096 WD, Fax : 45239.
Hours: Monday to Friday   08h30 - 14h30
               Saturday   08h30 - 11h00

BARCLAYS WELCOMES YOU TO SWAZILAND

- 12   Branches in Swaziland
- 70   Countries worldwide
- 370 Offices in Africa
- 1000 Ways to serve you

CALL US ON 42691

MERIDIEN BANK SWAZILAND LTD. P.O. BOX 261, EVENI, MBABANE,
Tel: 45401/3, Telex: 2380 WD, Fax: 44735
Hours: Monday to Friday   08h30 - 14h00
        Saturday   08h30 - 11h0

STANDARD CHARTERED BANK SWAZILAND LTD. P. O. BOX 68, MBABANE
Tel: 43351 Telex: 2220 WD, Fax: 44060
Hours: Monday, Tuesday,
        Thursday, Friday   08h30 - 14h30
        Wednesday   08h30 - 12h00
        Saturday   08h30 - 11h00

SWAZILAND DEVELOPMENT AND SAVINGS BANK. P. O. BOX 336, MBABANE.
Tel: 42551/8, Telex: 2055 WD. Fax: 41214
Hours: 1st - 21st of month   08h30 - 13h00
        22nd - last day of month   08h00 - 13h00
        Saturday   08h30 - 11h00
The Airport desk at Matsapha is open to cater for scheduled flights.

STANBIC BANK OF SWAZILAND LTD. P. O. BOX A294, SWAZI PLAZA, MBABANE.
Tel: 46589, 46592, 46596, Telex: 2216 WD, Fax: 45899
Hours: Monday to Friday   08h30 - 13h00
                              14h00 - 15h30
        Saturday   08h30 - 11h00

Standard Chartered Bank at Matsapha

A bridge between Africa and the world

Africa is about trade. Trade is about building bridges. In international banking, MERIDIEN BIAO is the bridge between Africa and the world.

From multinational corporations seeking increased market share to individuals and small businesses looking for joint ventures – MERIDIEN BIAO forges the link.

Putting people and companies together, providing the facilities and products that today's business demands, is second nature to us. Years of achievement in Africa based on local knowledge gives us the edge.

MERIDIEN BIAO delivers with all the sophistication expected from highly experienced banking professionals. All backed by a range of trade related services and products through the largest branch network of any bank in Africa.

Link your world with Africa – come over to the bank that built the bridge.

MERIDIEN BIAO.......
Africa is our business.

MERIDIEN BIAO
Bank Swaziland Limited

MERIDIEN BIAO House, West Street, Mbabane, PO Box 261, Eveni.
Tel: 45401/2/3. Fax: 44735. Telex: 2380 WD & 2166 WD

SOUTH AFRICAN REPRESENTATIVE OFFICE:
MXM House, 102 Rivonia Road, PO Box 78788, Sandton 2146, Johannesburg.
Tel: (11) 883 6740. Fax: (11) 884 4840. Telex: 095 450054 SA.

BRANCHES IN: **MBABANE, MANZINI, MATSAPHA.**

BANKS IN AFRICA:
BURKINA FASO, BURUNDI, CAMEROON, CENTRAL AFRICAN REPUBLIC, CHAD, EQUATORIAL GUINEA, GABON, GAMBIA, GHANA, KENYA, LIBERIA, MALI, NIGER, NIGERIA, SIERRA LEONE, SWAZILAND, TANZANIA, TOGO, ZAIRE, ZAMBIA.

OTHER OFFICES:
ABIDJAN · HAMBURG · LONDON · NEW YORK · PARIS.

The Swazi Plaza and Mall. Photo by Fotostudio

Replacement Tyres
Wheel Balancing
Puncture Repairs
Alignment
Mbabane: No 1 Karlyn Centre, Mbabane.
Tel: (09268) 46858/9
Matsapa: Mbabane-Manzini Road.
Tel: (09268) 54368/9

maxiprest TYRES

Swaziland Tyre Services

COMMERCIAL HOURS

Weekdays: 08h30 - 17h00   Saturdays: 08h30 - 13h00
Government offices are closed on Saturdays and most businesses close for lunch. Shops in general stay open throughout the day. Some of the larger supermarkets open on Sunday morning.

POST OFFICES

Normal post office services are available throughout the country. Visitors needing postage stamps may obtain these from their hotel or during the following hours:
Weekdays   08h00 - 16h00   Saturdays   :   08h00 - 11h00

PETROL HOURS

Generally petrol stations are open from 07h00 - 18h00. Many stations offer a service for 24 hours, especially those operating in the Ezulwini Valley and Mbabane. Fuel prices are often cheaper in Swaziland. It is wise to check the comparative costs before filling up.

GARAGES

The main agents in Swaziland are: **Coopers**: B.M.W.,VW, Audi, Landrover 41221/42363 **Leites**: Toyota 43536/53521. **Swazi Delta**: Opel, Suzuki, Isuzu 43501. **Tracar**: Mercedes, Nissan, Honda 40691/52461. Garages are generally open from 07h30 - 17h00 and closed on Saturdays. Spares for most makes of vehicles are readily available from the main dealers or from spares shops such as Midas in Mbabane and Manzini. Tyres, repairs and wheel balancing are undertaken by Swaziland Tyre Services (Maxiprest) in Mbabane and Manzini.

CHURCHES

Anglican

	Venue	Time	
Mbabane	All Saints, Edward St	06h30 08h00	English
		10h00	Siswati
Manzini	St. George & St. James	10h15, 18h00	English
Fairview Manzini	St. Pauls	09h00	SiSwati
Malkerns	Malkerns Valley	09h00	English
Pigg's Peak	St.Anne's	08h00	English
Nhlangano	Holy Trinity	08h00	English
Big Bend	Anglican Chapelry	07h00	English
Luyengo	Usuthu Mission Church	08h00	English

Catholic

	Venue	Time	
Manzini	Cathedral	Daily 05h30	English
		Sun 07h30, 09h00	English
Mbabane	Mater Delarosa Mission	Sun 08h00 17h00	English
		09h00	Portuguese
		10h00	SiSwati

Methodist

	Venue	Time	
Manzini	Fairview	10h15	English
Mbabane		09h00, 10h00	SiSwati
Malkerns		09h00	SiSwati

Lutheran

	Venue	Time	
Manzini	Lutheran Centre	08h30	English

HOSPITALS

			FIRE/ EMERGENCY	
Mbabane Clinic Service	42423		Mbabane	43333
Mbabane Government Hospital	42111		Manzini	53333
Raleigh Fitkin Hospital Manzini	52211		Lobamba	61333
Pigg's Peak Government Hospital	71111		Siteki	34333
Baphalali Red Cross	42532		Nhlangano	78333

POLICE

Emergency	999	Siteki	34222
Mbabane	42221	Airport/Police	84220
Manzini	52221	Piggs Peak	71222
Lobamba	61221	Nhlangano	78222
Malkerns	83011	Simunye	38223
Big Bend	36322	Bhunya	74222

Visitors should be vigilant over their personal belongings and valuables, although Swaziland is generally safe and secure, the Police strongly advise that items of value should be locked away in hotel safes or in the boot of your car and not left in evidence for possible pilferage.

Colourful traditional crafts at Mbabane Craft Market. Photo by Fotostudio

SERVICE CLUBS

Rotary	Venue	Day	Time
Rotary Club of Malkerns	Malandela's	Tuesday	18h00
Rotary Club of Manzini	Enjabulweni	Monday	19h00
Rotary Club of Mbabane	Mountain Inn	Friday	13h00
Rotary Club of Mbabane Mbuluzi	Mountain Inn	Thursday	18h15

Round Table

Mbabane Round Table	Sifundzane School	2nd Tuesday	18h30
Manzini Round Table	Manzini Club	1st & 3rd Thurs	19h30
Piggs Peak, Bulembu	Peak Timbers	1st Tues	19h00
Simunye, Ehlanzeni	Own Club House	1st & 3rd Thurs.	19h00

Lions Club

Manzini Lions Club	Enjabulweni	1st Thurs	18h30/ 19h00
Mbabane Lions Club	Mountain Inn	4th Tues	19h00

ASSISTANCE GROUPS

There are no recognised assistance associations in the Kingdom, however, there are informal groups and individuals who are able to assist. Contact Telephone No: 55490 or 45924. For those visitors who are in need of more structured counsel and help, the following organizations are to be found in Johannesburg. Telephone code from Swaziland (07 - 11)

Alcoholics Anonymous	337 7870	Life Line	728 1347

SPORTING FACILITIES

Golf

Swaziland has some of the most spectacular golf courses in the world. Just to walk in this majestic scenery whilst enjoying a 9 or 18 hole game is truly therapeutic. The Royal Swazi Sun 18 hole golf course is championship class, and run by the Swaziland Golf Club. Major tournaments are played regularly at the Royal Swazi course including PRO-AM and the King's Trophy.

Another good 18 hole course is to be found at the Mbabane Golf Club only 2 kms from the city centre on Allister Miller Street leading north towards Pine Valley. The 9 hole course at the Manzini Golf Course on the Ngwane Road leading towards Siteki is a further popular venue.

Country golf courses include: Bulembu Golf Club near Piggs Peak, Mhlume Country Club and Simunye Country Club in the North East of Swaziland, the Usutu Club in the West and the Siteki Club in the Lowveld, also at the Shiselweni Country Club which is very close to the Nhlangano Sun Hotel and Casino in the south of the Kingdom.

Royal Swazi Sun Golf	61001	Simunye Country Club	38182
Bulembu/Havelock	73214	Manzini Golf Club	52254
Mbabane Golf Club	42285	Shiselweni/Nhlangano Su	78211

Tennis

Tennis courts of a very high standard are to be found at the Royal Swazi Sun, the Ezulwini Sun and the Yen Saan Hotel in the Ezulwini Valley. In Pigg's Peak there are excellent tennis courts at the Protea Pigg's Peak Hotel and Casino. The Forester's Arms in Mhlambanyati has its own court. The Nhlangano Sun also has a court Arms

World under one flag.

Is the reason for our customers success in dealing internationally the fact that Stanbic Bank is a dynamic bank with a link to more than 2 000 correspondent banks worldwide? That we have the vast experience of a major Regional bank at our fingertips?

Is it that we have access to the sophisticated electronic communications systems that gives our customers a more efficient and accurate service whatever the complexities of the transactions?

Or is it the fact that we offer a wide range of international banking products and services, backed up by the expertise of specialist international bankers who tailor our services to your unique requirements?

We believe that it is all these.

Head office: PO Box A294, Swazi Plaza, Mbabane, Swaziland. Telephone : (09268) 46587 /589/ 592/ 596. Fax: (09268) 45899.

International Trade Centre: PO Box A294, Swazi Plaza, Mbabane, Swaziland. Telephone: (09268)46587/589/592/596. Fax: (09268) 44747. Telex: 2216 WD.

Formerly UnionBank of Swaziland Ltd.
A member of the Standard Bank Group of South Africa.

With us you can go so much further.

in Mhlambanyati has its own court. National tennis courts can be found at the Swaziland College of Technology and Coronation Park in Mbabane. Country Clubs include tennis among their facilities, the above telephone numbers will assist visitors in checking availability of courts to non-members. In addition, Malkerns Country Club on 83018 have a tennis court, visitors should ensure that they are welcome as non-members and be prepared to pay the required court fee.

Horse Riding/Stables

Horse riding is a wonderful way to explore Swaziland. Areas of the Kingdom which are totally inaccessible by car become part of the Swaziland experience on the back of a horse. There are a number of riding stables which offer outrides, riding lessons and riding camps for the young.

Mlilwane Wildlife Sanctuary includes game viewing from horseback which is truly a close encounter with nature.

The Forester's Arms and Meikles Mount Estate in Mhlambanyati are set in the horse trailing country of the Usutu Forests. Horses may be hired by the hour to enjoy the magnificent scenery of the west of Swaziland. Horse riding is available at the Sun International Hotels in the Ezulwini Valley and Protea Pigg's Peak Hotel & Casino.

Stables.

Mlilwane Wildlife Sanctuary	61037	Sun International (residents)	61001
Forester's Arms Hotel (residents)	74177	Protea Pigg's Peak Hotel (residents)	71104
Meikles Mount Estate (residents)	74110	Hawana, Malolotja	24109/42619
Pine Tree, Ezulwini	61484	Nyanza, Malkerns	83090

Bowls

Bowls and bowls tournaments are very popular within the Kingdom. The Royal Swazi Sun has two superb bowling greens and the Protea Pigg's Peak Hotel also offer bowls as one of the many sporting facilities. Other Bowling greens can be found at the Country Clubs.

Squash

The Royal Swazi Sun has 2 excellent squash courts. Protea Pigg's Peak Hotel which is recently built, have 2 air-conditioned, glass backed courts for resident's use. Private courts may be found at the Manzini Club and Coronation Park in Mbabane.

Fishing

Swaziland's well watered soil fed by its many rivers offers very good fishing for the angler. The Usutu Forests are inter-crossed with rivers carrying rainbow trout. Fishing is plentiful and visitors at the Forester's Arms may obtain permits to fish in the forest waters. In addition, indigenous fish including bream, yellowfish, barbel, mud fish and eels are found in most rivers. Meikles Mount at Mhlambanyati have bordering rivers to their estates which are well stocked with indigenous fish. Permits to fish are free but must be obtained. Contact the Ministry of Agriculture offices, P.O. Box 162, Mbabane.

Swimming

Most of the hotels have their own swimming pools and many cater for children with a second shallow pool. It is wiser to avoid swimming in the rivers, as they may be bilharzia infested. However fast flowing streams are usually safe. Phophonyane Lodge swimming pool is natural clear water and very safe.

FOREIGN REPRESENTATIVES RESIDENT IN SWAZILAND

**European Community
Delegation of the Commission**
of the European Communities
3rd Floor, Dhlan'ubeka House,
P.O. Box A36, Swazi Plaza, Mbabane
Tel: 42908, 44769, 22191.
Telex: 2133 WD, Fax: 46729
Delegate: Mr. Gabriel Lee

The Royal Belgian Consulate
P.O. Box,33, Eveni, Mbabane
Tel: 46089 or 83403 (private)
Hon Consul: Mr. Xavier Gobin

The Royal Danish Consulate
Ground Floor, Sokhamlilo Building,
Johnson St, Mbabane.
P.O. Box 815, Mbabane.
Tel 43547, Telex 2018 WD.Fax 43548
Hon Consul: Mr Hans Noddeboe

Embassy of Israel
Mbabane House, Warner Street,
P.O. Box 146, Mbabane
Tel: 42626, Fax: 45857
Ambassador: Mr.Pinchas Lavie

The Italian Consulate
219,Tenbergen St, Manzini,
P.O. Box 928, Manzini
Tel: 52436 Telex 2241 Wd Fax 52436
Consul: Mr Marsio D'Orsi

Embassy of the Republic of Germany
3rd Floor Dhlan'ubeka House, Mbabane,
P.O. Box 1507, Tel: 43174,Telex: 3021 WD
Liaison Officer: Ms Angelina Topfer

Embassy of the Republic of South Africa,
Allister Miller Street, Mbabane,
P.O. Box 2507, Mbabane,
Tel: 44651, Telex: 2341 WD, Fax: 46944
Ambassador: Mr. I .Heath

British High Commission
Allister Miller St, Mbabane
Private Bag Mbabane
Tel:42581/3 , Fax: 42585
Commissioner: Mr. Richard Gozney

Embassy of the United States of America
Central Bank Building,, Warner St,
P.O. Box 199,Mbabane
Tel: 46441/2, Fax: 45959
Ambassador: Mr. John Sprott

Embassy of the People's Republic of Mozambiqe
Princess Drive, Mbabane
P.O. Box 1212, Mbabane,Tel: 43700
Te;ex 2248 WD, Fax: 43692,
Ambassador: Mr. Antonio Sumbana

Consulate of the Netherlands
Business Machines House, Mbabane,
P.O. Box 1205, Mbabane
Tel: 45178, 45884, Fax: 44006
Hon. Consul: Mr Frederik Oostergetel

Portuguese Consulate
Portuguese Club, O.K. Road, Mbabane,
P.O. Box 855, Mbabane,
Tel: 46780. Telex: 2379 WD, Fax: 46770
Hon. Consul: Mr Carlos de M. Lopes

Embassy of the Republic of China
Warner Street, Mbabane, P.O. Box 56,
Tel: 42379, Telex: 2167 WD,Fax: 46688
Ambassador: Mr. Enti Liu

Consulate of Austria,
P.O.Box 282, Malkerns,
Tel: 52105
Consul: Mr. G. Albrecht

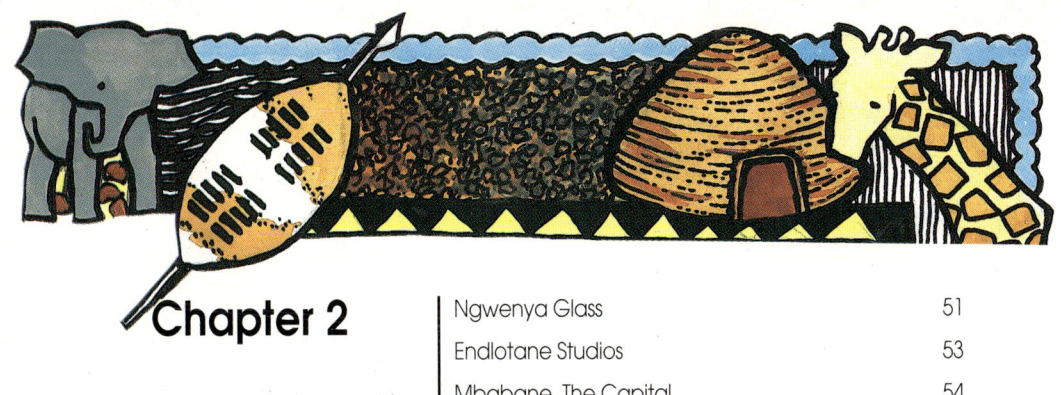

Chapter 2

The Journey from Oshoek/Ngwenya to Mbabane

Ngwenya Glass	51
Endlotane Studios	53
Mbabane, The Capital	54
The Tavern Hotel	54
The City Inn	55
Mbabane Market	56
The Swazi Plaza	59
The Mall and The New Mall	61, 65
The Mountain Inn	69
The Swazi Inn	70

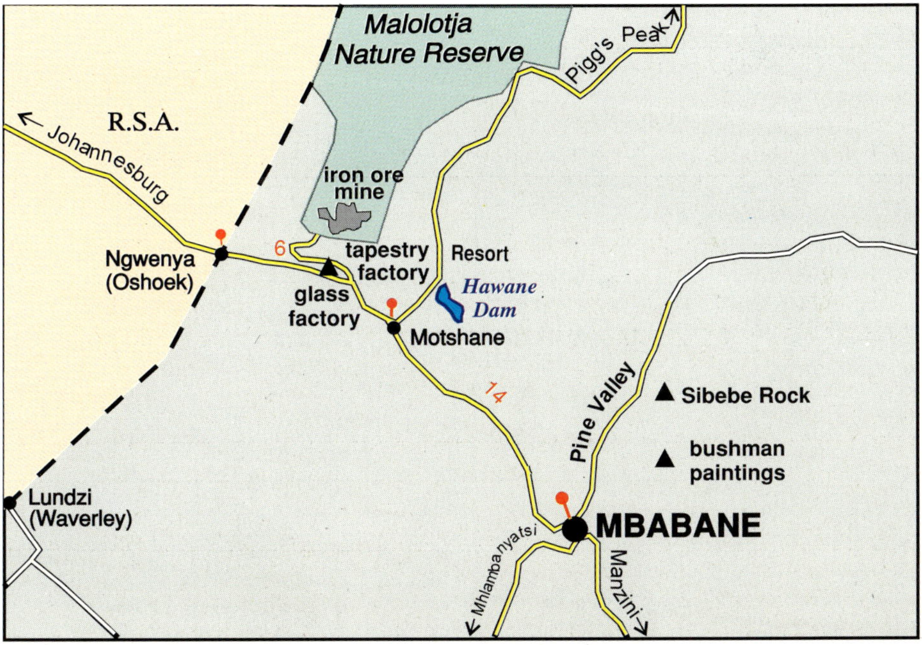

NGWENYA GLASS

MANUFACTURERS OF HAND MADE GLASSWARE
GLASSES, ORNAMENTAL ITEMS, TABLEWARE
AFRICAN ANIMALS, FIGURES ETC.

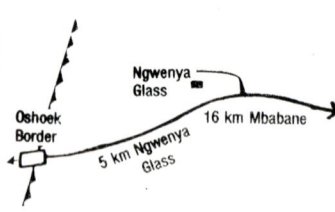

The only factory in Africa specializing in handmade glass. Visitors welcome to see our Swazi craftsmen at work and choose a souvenir at factor prices from our well stocked showroom.

Showroom and Coffee Shop
Open 7 days a week
9.00am - 3.30pm

P.O. Box 45,
Motshane, Swaziland.
Tel: 24053, 24151, 24142
Fax: all above and ask.

The new Showroom

The upstairs Coffee Shop

THE JOURNEY FROM OSHOEK/NGWENYA TO MBABANE

The Oshoek/Ngwenya border is the most popular crossing point to the Kingdom. Immigration formalities include completion of forms on the South African side and further forms at the Swaziland immigration and customs points. The new Swaziland border post facilitates smoother entry to the Kingdom. Once you are in Swaziland, you can enjoy the magnificent scenery from the border to Mbabane. Only metres from the border post, the visitor comes upon a handicraft centre on the left from where rustic arts are sold by Swazi women. This is an opportunity for the visitor to assess Swazi crafts from the indigenous level and to explore the range of products which are available.

Travel approximately 5 kms from the border and take the turning to the left pointing to Ngwenya Glass and Endlotane Studios/Phumalanga Tapestries.

NGWENYA GLASS

Ngwenya Glass is the only glass making factory of its kind in the Southern hemisphere. Swazi glass-blowers fashion individual pieces into delicate animal shapes, table glass ware, ornaments and souvenirs. The basic glass is recycled from clear glass and each piece is original, crafted by skilled Swazi glass blowers and engravers to make a special item for you to take home. During the week you may watch the glass blowers at work, by standing on a balcony overlooking the workshop floor, the visitor may watch each piece passed from the originator through subsequent stages until the final glass piece is ready for sale. This is rustic glassware, individual to Swaziland where each piece is made with great care and the final product may be a pair of bookends, a large elephant or a simple paperweight, all made from recycled glass. Ngwenya Glass are committed to wildlife conservation; a percentage of their sales is donated to the "Save the Rhino Fund". The glass factory was originally opened in 1979 by Swedish Craftsmen. After some difficult years, the present owners the Prettejohn family bought the business in 1987. Since that time Ngwenya Glass has grown from strength to strength. Master Glass-blower, Sibusiso Mhlanga, who was trained by the Swedes, remains the leading craftsman at Ngwenya, he in turn has trained further glass-blowers who together make a wide variety of tableware and glass ornaments. The very attractive glass tableware, particularly the wine glasses are both functional and original; a resident engraver will execute various designs or engrave your name upon a special glass souvenir. Ngwenya Glass have established a sister glass making factory in Johannesburg called "Shades of Ngwenya" which makes shades, vases and salad bowls, some of these products are now on display. A new coffee-shop is situated upstairs serving a choice of coffees or teas, savoury or sweet pancakes, scones, ice-creams and cool drinks. Ngwenya Glass is exported worldwide. Many prestigious country lodges and hotels are set with Ngwenya Glass; fruit bowls, vases and ashtrays have been ordered for Sun International to furnish their many hotels including the recently revamped venues at Sun City. Browse around and return to Ngwenya Glass, on each occasion you will find something new and different. **Showroom open daily from 9.00am - 4.00pm. Ngwenya Glass, Tel: 24053/24151/24142, Fax: same numbers and request.**

ENDLOTANE STUDIOS

TAPESTRIES   WOODCRAFT   POTTERY   PRINTING

**Studios and showroom
Mbabane/Oshoek Road
former Iron Ore Buildings, Ngwenya
P.O. Box A463, Swazi Plaza, Mbabane,
Kingdom of Swaziland.**

Tel: (268) 45447/9
Fax : (268) 45449

Entrance to the Lion Cavern at Ngwenya

The Nkomati River enroute to Piggs Peak

ENDLOTANE STUDIOS/PHUMALANGA TAPESTRIES

Continue a further kilometre and follow the signs to Endlotane Studios/Phumalanga Tapestries. The Reck family began Swaziland Tapestries in 1974. Artist and originator Albert Christoph Reck designs the patterns for exquisite tapestries depicting African history, bushmen paintings and modern, colourful artistry. The visitor may watch the whole process from carding of mohair Merino wool, to spinning the yarn, dying each piece in delicate shades and then the weaving. Guaranteed for life, the Endlotane Studios woven article is internationally recognised by the Phumalanga Swazihand trademark. Limited editions are made of selected designs and every tapestry is accompanied by a certificate authenticating ownership and a brief description of the origin of the work.

Not only a tapestry workshop, Endlotane Studios also specialise in hand made, contemporary furniture. Delicately dyed wood, coupled with subtle fabrics make up unusual chairs, settees and occasional furniture. In addition they collect the different craft artefacts which complement their tapestries and furnishings. Orders for individual designs are taken and the finished works are exported all over the world. The artistry of Albert Christoph Reck complements the crafts of the Swazi women who weave the tapestries. Designs are drawn onto huge patterns, nimble fingers follow the pattern to bring life and colour to the work. There are workshops for the development of art design, to incorporate stone cutters and the creation of textiles for interior decoration and a tea-room to give visitors time to browse and consider. Their artistry is really unique and a tapestry from Endlotane is a piece of art to treasure forever.

Endlotane Studios, Tel: 45447/9, Fax: 45449. Open Daily: 8.00am - 5.00pm

Return to the main road, turn left towards Mbabane which at this point is 17 kms away. Travel a further 2 kms and note the road to the left pointing to Pigg's Peak (see chapter 8). The continuing journey to Mbabane is awesome in its beauty. This is the Highveld of Swaziland with its majestic mountains, sharply dropping escarpments and stark outlines. Be careful of crossing cattle and goats, yet enjoy the endless ranges of hilltops as you drop towards the capital. Be sure to obey the 80 kph speed limit and be aware of the 60 kph signs as you approach Mbabane. At the signpost pointing towards the city centre to the left, turn left and travel along Gilfillan Street towards the main centre of town. If you continue along the by-pass road, this brings you to the central traffic lights and turn-off towards the Ezulwini Valley and Manzini.

Endlotane Studio tapestries, furniture and furnishings

- "Jubilee Room"
  A la carte Restaurant
- Conference Facilities
- Swimming Pool
- Function Rooms
- Television in all Rooms
- Sporting Facilities • Golf
- Fully Furnished Apartment to Rent

Tel: 42361/2, Fax: 40373, Telex: 2306 WD
P.O. Box 25, Mbabane. Swaziland

The Tavern Hotel. Photo by Fotostudio

MBABANE THE CAPITAL

We are now exploring Mbabane which is a cosmopolitan city and the governmental centre of the Kingdom. Foreign Embassies maintain their offices in Mbabane and most commercial head offices are established in the capital. The City Council is determined to improve the municipal services in the city and private enterprise has joined hand in hand with local government to develop shopping trading areas.

Background

Tradition suggests that Mbabane was named after a local chief; the name means "something sharp and bitter" which may reflect the personality of the chief rather than the character of the capital. Mbabane developed near a cattle station upon which sweet grass known as "lulubane" grew, this name probably became "Mbabane" in which the final vowel is pronounced softly. The town was founded as the administrative capital in 1902 by the colonial government primarily because of its altitude, its location beneath the Dlangeni hills and its temperate climate. Mbabane has approximately 80,000 inhabitants and is rapidly expanding.

Travel along Gilfillan Street passing the SCOT centre and the veterinarian offices. At the junction with Allister Miller Street turn off right towards The Tavern Hotel.

THE TAVERN HOTEL

40 ensuite rooms with T.V 8 poolside rooms. Swimming pool and squash court and within close proximity to golf, tennis and bowls. A fully furnished apartment is also available to visitors. The Tavern has an open air business venue known as "Fern

Court" which attracts after business clientele who wish to relax and exchange ideas over cocktails. The "Fern Court" offers quality, light refreshments, good company and the opportunity for discreet conversation. The Tavern is primarily a business hotel, this new extension is for early evening professional clientele and can be a lively centre for visitors seeking the pulse of the city. There is a well equipped conference and business centre utilised for seminars, meetings and tutorials.

This old English style hotel, faced with timber and situated on an elevated position overlooking the city, offers a warm reception and an opportunity to meet city residents at leisure. The Jubilee Restaurant is noted for continental fare within an intimate atmosphere. The Tavern's central situation lends itself as a good venue for business visitors who may need conference facilities with a back up secretarial service.

Bookings: Tavern Hotel, Box 25, Mbabane Tel: 42361/2, 42568/9, 42454, Telex: 2306 WD. Fax: 40373

Within walking distance is the Swaziland Theatre Club which produces dramas, comedies and musicals every quarter. The Cinelux cinema is also close by as is the main street of Mbabane, Allister Miller Street, named after the first proprietor of the Times of Swaziland daily newspaper. Allister Miller (senior) transported the original printing press from Delgoa Bay (Maputo) to start this first newspaper.

Turn left onto Allister Miller Street and travel a short way towards the Mbabane Club and Golf Course on your right. Visitors may use the Golf Club amenities on payment of a green fee. Enquire at the Mbabane Club regarding bowls, squash and tennis facilities for non-members. Travel further along the Golf Course Road and you will discover the residential areas of Mbabane and the Mbuluzi River which flows through Pine Valley. There are some waterfalls in this area which should not be missed.

Waterfalls at Pine Valley . Photo by Fotostudio

CITY INN

23 ensuite Double Rooms recently refurbished. Centrally situated Pablo's all day Restaurant, Pele's pool room and bar. Secure Parking.

Towards the end of Allister Miller Street on the right is the newly renovated City Inn. The

CITY INN

Allister Miller Street, Mbabane, Swaziland
Telephone: (+268) 42034/42406
Fax: (+268) 45855

City Inn is owned and managed by the family who run the Mountain Inn, already this exciting hotel has a special air of professionalism which should mark any good city hotel. Situated right in the middle of the capital, close to shops, banks, Ministries, commercial houses, the gym and aerobics centre, the cinema, theatre and sporting facilities, It is ideal for busy guests who need to be at the centre of activity and commerce. Taxis are on call and secretarial services can be arranged for visiting businessmen. "Pablo's" the all day restaurant which fronts onto Allister Miller Street, serves breakfast, lunch and dinner as well as a good snack choice; there is a take away service and inhouse service.

Bookings: City Inn, P. O. Box 15, Mbabane, Tel: 42406/42034, Fax: 42034/45855

MBABANE MARKET

Two minutes walk from the City Inn and across Msunduza Street brings you to the Mbabane Market. Here you will find an assortment of basketware, stone and wood carvings, ethnic sculptures, hats, T-shirts and sisal mats. Sellers expect to haggle, so brush up on your persuasive skills to strike a bargain. Alongside the handicraft market is Mbabane's fruit and vegetable market replete with fresh vegetables and fruit from the Kingdom. Huge pineapples, bananas, citrus, guavas and mangoes are for sale in season. Take time browsing around these stalls, there are some bargains toenjoy.

From the Mbabane Market, turn right and walk along Msunduza Street. On the left is the Mbabane Library with a good Reference section. Visitors who wish to learn more of the history, geography and culture of Swaziland will find the library staff very helpful. Opposite the Library is the Central Bank and next to this is the Embassy of the Republic of China; an oriental building in red and green which reminds the visitor of the international ingredients contributing to the fabric of this delightful Kingdom.

DISCOVER
INDINGILIZI GALLERY
& COURTYARD RESTAURANT
(SERVING AFRICAN DISHES)
ART GALLERY - PICTURE FRAMERS

Alternating exhibitions.
Selected arts, hand crafted furniture,
batiks, baskets, African jewellery.
Large choice of quality
Rosecraft mohair. Stockists of
art materials and
SO MUCH MORE!!

112, JOHNSON STREET
P.O. BOX 326, MBABANE, Swaziland
TELEPHONE 46213 FAX 46404

L.M.
RESTAURANT

..at the main 5-way junction, next to
Mbabane Motors centre of
Mbabane
Gilfillan Street
Continental Cuisine
Seafood specialities
Wide selection of wines
Excellent service

Telephone 43097

WEBSTERS BOOKSTORES AND VIDEOS.

Webster's bookshops are long established within Swaziland particularly as suppliers and distributors of educational books. During the heavy rains of summer, Webster's staff overcome flooded rivers and deep mud in order to deliver school books on time. Browse around their shop in Johnson Street for informative and light literature, periodicals and newspapers. Webster's video shop is on Allister Miller Street opposite the Cinelux cinema. A fine selection of up to the minute films are available. Websters also have a shop in the newly opened New Mall known as "Book and Pen".

Websters, Tel: 42560,42242, Fax: 44897. Videos, Tel: 45386. Book and Pen, Tel: 46619

INDINGILIZI ART GALLERY

In Johnson Street, is Indigilizi Art Gallery a treasure chest of creative art, crafts, artists materials, carvings, mohair, batiks, jewellery and some very unusual old beadwork. Picture mounting and framing is a speciality of this art gallery. Owner and artist Dorie Angus-Verhoog travels widely to find the unusual and best in African art. An al fresco restaurant adjoins the gallery serving ethnic dishes from Cape to Cairo every lunch time.
**Indingilizi Art Gallery and African Courtyard Restaurant.
Tel: 46213, Fax: 46213**

*The Indingilizi African Courtyard Restaurant
Photo by Fotostudio*

L.M. RESTAURANT

Diagonally opposite the Tavern Hotel on a prominent site overlooking Allister Miller Street is the well established L.M. Restaurant. The L.M. has a distinctly Continental atmosphere, tables are placed in individual booths and the fare is Portuguese with a Mozambican flavour. King and Queen prawns, chicken peri-peri, spicey chicken livers in addition to a wide range of fish, meat and chicken dishes are served. The L.M. keeps a good range of Portuguese and South African wines to accompany well cooked food in an easy, informal atmosphere.

L.M. Restaurant, Tel: 43097

Marco's Trattoria. Photo by Fotostudio

Marco's Trattoria

Pizza, Pasta & Grills

FULLY LICENSED
Allister Miller Street,
Mbabane
Telephone: (268) 45029

MARCO'S TRATTORIA

Marco's Trattoria is a very popular Italian restaurant situated on Allister Miller Street on the right overlooking the street. A very popular venue for families, young couples and business lunches, Marco's has a cosy, confidential ambience. The upstairs location gives it an air of being apart from the bustle of the city. The selection of dishes is wide ranging from fish, chicken, steaks and, of course, pasta and pizzas. Recently refurbished and extended to include dining on the balconies and a secluded area for business discussions, Marco's is fully licensed and a very welcoming restaurant for the visitor to discover and enjoy.

Marco's Trattoria, Tel: 45029

The Mediterranean Restaurant

THE MEDITERRANEAN RESTAURANT
FULLY LICENCED

Allister Miller Street
(Opposite Cinelux Cinema)
P.O. Box 695, Mbabane, Swaziland
Telephone: (+268) 43212

"Indian Cuisine"

"Home of Halal Food"

Various curries, prawns, grills, seafoods and snacks.

Open Everyday
10.30 am-12.00 pm

THE MEDITERRANEAN RESTAURANT

Further along Allister Miller Street, almost opposite the Cinelux Cinema is one of Mbabane best kept secrets. This delightful, secluded restaurant offers a variety of dishes including curries, grills and seafoods. It is owner managed and is the ideal place to visit before or after the cinema show. A fully licensed bar is within the restaurant area and subdued llighting and intimate booths are perfect for friendly, social celebrations. Good selection of South African and Portuguese wines is offered. A takeway service is available and all food is Halal.

Mediterranean Restaurant, Tel: 43212

THE SWAZI PLAZA

No visit to Mbabane is complete without exploring the Swazi Plaza. This is a pedestrian precinct of shops, coffee houses, banks, supermarkets and departmental stores set within one complex. Modern shops and select boutiques offer the visitor high fashion wear or ethnic originality. Bookshops, Interior design shops, curios and souvenirs, shoes, chemist, accessory and gift shops, photo lab ,intimate coffee shops and bars tempt the visitor to linger. A new wing has recently been completed which houses the new offices of Stanbic Bank. Stanbic have amalgamated all of their staff under one roof and include a fully equipped training centre, foreign exchange dealing and a Reuters dish to receive instant communications. Longhorn Restaurant has opened to delight hungry diners.

PHILANI AND MBABANE PHARAMCIES

The Swazi Plaza. Photo by Fotostudio

Opposite the O.K. Bazaar supermarket is a very well-stocked chemist which specialises in medicines and toiletries for the visitor. Suntan oils and sunscreen creams, after swimming lotions, smooth sliding bath and shower gels and lots of lovely, sweet smelling toiletries to pamper you whilst on holiday are all to be found here. Anti-malaria tablets, upset tummy remedies and medicines for the children are to hand plus plenty of professional advice from the resident pharmacist. A sister shop is located in Allister Miller Street; buy your cosmetics and personal toiletries when in Swaziland, you may be pleasantly surprised by the choice, variety and price.

Philani Pharmacy, Tel: 46460, Mbabane Pharmacy, Tel: 42817

LUCIANO
MENS BOUTIQUE

In Fashion for Men

Tel: (268) 45987 / 41557 Swazi Plaza, Mbabane
Tel: (268) 55222, Bhunu Mall, Manzini
Kingdom of Swaziland

LUCIANO MENS BOUTIQUE

Placed in a prominent location of the Swazi Plaza is Luciano Mens Boutique, an up market shop which caters for every possible requirement of the well dressed man. Top brands and designs are sold here from Yves St. Laurent, Christian Dior, Polo, Givenchy, Dormeiul and Viyella ensuring the very best in cut, cloth and colour. Colourful sports and leisure wear, muted tones for the more formal business suit, superb cut and material for evening wear; all are here, so much choice, such great quality from this high fashion shop. Don't forget to buy some exotic aftershave or French perfume for your partner; Luciano have an extensive range of the top brands.
Luciano Mens Boutique, Tel: 45987, 41557, Fax: 41557.

FOTORAMA

Located next to the Swazi Plaza Post Office, close to Barclays Bank, the National Airline, a leading travel agent and two restaurants is a highly efficient photographic processing lab and shop. Fotorama offer a same day service for slide processing and 1 hour colour print processing for both postcard and Jumbo prints, enlargements of your holiday photos and as many re-prints as you want. Why not send a photo of your holiday to relatives and friends, this can be more personal than a postcard? Stock up on slide and print films and photo accessories from this friendly shop which is owner managed, professionally run and takes extreme personal care of your films.
Fotorama, Tel: 44250, Fax: 42485

Fotorama at the Swazi Plaza. Photo by Fotostudio

Inside Living in Africa. Photo by Fotostudio

LIVING IN AFRICA

Well located at the Plaza is an interior design and decor shop, "Living in Africa". This is a unique, good looking shop which provides inspiration for home interiors with an African flavour. "Living in Africa" is a treasure trove containing specific areas to highlight interior decor, furnishings, glass and table ware and contemporary furniture. Ideas for presents abound and there is a kitchen corner filled with articles from all parts of the world. Coral Steven's mohair is displayed in swathes of beautifully muted and combined colours. No expense has been spared to make this very attractive shop into a haven for those seeking ideas, gifts or advice on their home decor. Swazi glass, candles, pottery, mohair and fabric blend with wicker, steel, glass and ethnic furniture. Pretty decorative tableware, imported from Europe and South Africa, slender table candles, ethnic printed tablecloths and napkins, attractive table lamps, pictures from the Southern African region and decorative table mats are all here for the buyer to browse among, choose and take home as an apt souvenir.

Living in Africa, Tel: 46468, Fax: 43021

THE MALL

The River Mbabane runs through the valley of the city separating the older, higher part of the capital from the new shopping area. An exciting centre next to the River Mbabane is The Mall which lies opposite the Swazi Plaza across the OK Road. The shopping malls are constructed under domed glass which allows natural light to enter the area beneath. A number of highly unusual shops are here including fashion boutiques, accessory and shoe shops, a sports shop, luggage shop, interior decor shop, photo lab, camera and electronic goods shop, an exclusive designer menswear shop, hair and beauty salon and chemist plus international franchise operations and top class restaurants invite the visitor to explore and enjoy. This centre runs regular street markets, small bazaars and has a tremendous pull for local residents and visitors. Every weekend, the buzz happens at the Mall.

SPAR SUPERMARKET

Standing prominently as the Anchor shop of the Mall is Spar Supermarket, a wonderful shop full of every possible food choice the visitor may need. From everyday food choices, to detergents and pet foods, Spar also has a well stocked section devoted to imported, luxury items, good teas, German and Swiss chocolates, tinned mussels, salmon and escargot, breakfast marmalades and jams, shortbread, chutneys and soups. The in-house bakery offers fresh bread, rolls, pastries and cakes 7 days a week plus those special wholemeal and health breads. A wine department stocks good South African wines from cellar boxes to more expensive choices. Stop at the delicatessen for a wholesome roll, imported cheese or a slice of ham. Spar Supermarket is open on Sunday morning when the Sunday papers are in stock, this is a good time to choose something different, meet with local residents and enjoy shopping at leisure before going on to one of the restaurants for Sunday lunch.

The Mall. Photo by Fotostudio

Spar Supermarket, Tel: 40571 Fax: 46023

..how lucky you are to have a friendly

SPAR

at The Mall in Mbabane
and at The Hub in Manzini
Come visit us soon!
Tel: 40571/2, Fax: 46023, P.O. Box 112
Mbabane, Swaziland

African Fantasy at the Mall

AFRICAN FANTASY

The Bock family have recently purchased the delightful shop at the Mall called "African Fantasy" which is a show place for all of the Armstrong Artworks products and much more. This is a fantastic place to browse; children love the enormous tree "planted" in the centre of the shop which houses monkeys, snakes and birds. The windows are full of "Armstrong" animals from the leopard, giraffe and gorilla to the smaller birds. From the wide range of T-shirts, especially the "Wild African Cat" range in both black and white and coloured the choice of the unusual is wide; there are colour-in posters complete with pens, look out for the "African Days" and "African Fantasy" posters which feature life in Swaziland, pencil boxes, colourful anoraks and sweat shirts, pottery mugs, tea-sets and ornamental plates, hand-made jewellery and greetings cards. This is a shop to really enjoy and have fun in.

African Fantasy, Tel: 40205

T-shirts, sweatshirts,
colour-in posters, cards,
writing papers, mugs, plates, tiles,
table cloths, T-towels
and much more!

African Fantasy
Shop 11, The Mall
Mbabane.
Kingdom of Swaziland
Tel (+268) 40205, 61244

FOR THE FINEST IN DINING PLEASURE....
LOOK NO FURTHER THAN

LA CASSEROLE

Mbabane
Tel: 46426

Fully licensed and serving the finest German and cosmopolitan cuisine individually prepared to order.

LA CASSEROLE

La Casserole is a well established restaurant offering excellent fare, a sophisticated ambiance and quality sevice. Fully licensed, La Casserole has a small inside bar to tempt the palette before having lunch or evening dinner. Inside the restaurant the decor is cool, spacious and professional, the wood panelling, wall photographs, table linen and flowers present an atmosphere of tranquillity which is extremely popular with local business diners and busy shoppers looking for a quiet haven and a good meal. The Restaurant has established a reputation as a leading venue for business lunches, morning and afternoon tea rendezvous and a romantic evening spot. There is a pizza oven for homemade, filling and tasty pizzas and in summer the outside patio resembles a German Beer garden where families and friends meet for a quiet drink or a party. Come and enjoy the Continental atmosphere of this spacious, charming restaurant, a cold beer or glass of wine is a fine way to end a busy day and look forward to a first class dinner.

La Casserole Restaurant, Tel: 46426

La Casserole. Photo by Fotostudio

The intimate bar at La Casserole.
Photo by Fotostudio

The New Mall. Photo by Fotostudio

THE NEW MALL

Leave the Mall and cross the bridge over the river Mbabane to the newly opened New Mall. This development is a wonderful extension to the existing marketing centres creating a new shopping experience for the people of Swaziland. The anchor shop is Woolworths with sister store Truworths flanking the entrance to the New Mall. The concept is light, airy and colourful with attractive hanging baskets, plants, lamp posts and a resident pianist plays to entertain and encourage shoppers and window gazers. Shops include Sunny Bananas; a fun shop attracting all who enjoy the unusual, imaginative and original; small, quality fashion boutiques, a kitchen kiosk, hardware store, confectionery kiosk, Chinese fashion and souvenirs, a fabric shop, book and newspaper shop and a well placed, upmarket jewellers. Two major food stores are within this complex; the well known, franchise Nando's and a large Chinese takeaway Kowloon. A great expansion for Mbabane and a further good reason for visitors to stay longer and enjoy the very latest shopping ideas.

The New Mall stages regular exhibitions, fun days and jamborees, all add entertainment to this new, exciting centre.

Art exhibition at the New Mall

MINISTRY OF TOURISM

Swaziland with its Culture, Tradition and Beautiful Scenic Surroundings.

Information to tourists on Accommodation, Hotels and Casinos, Nature and Games Reserves, Craft Centres and Shops and Tours to places of interest. Everything you may need to know about Swaziland.

TOURIST OFFICES
at
Swazi Plaza Mbabane, Swaziland
Tel: (268) 42531
and
Oshoek/Ngwenya Border Post
Tel: 24206

Ministry of Broadcasting, Information & Tourism
PO Box 338, Mbabane, Kingdom of Swaziland
Tel: (+268) 44556   Fax: (+268) 42774

Leave The Mall and travel along the OK Road to the Mbabane by-pass. Turn left and continue through the main traffic lights to the end of the dual carriageway. Turn left and immediately right passing the Mbabane Post Office on your right. Turn left again into Walker Street, on your right is a large 6 story building known as " Dlanu'beka House ", on the ground floor your will find the " Hwa Li Restaurant ".

THE HWA LI

A town restaurant with a difference, the Hwa Li is a Chinese Restaurant where the chef is Taiwanese and the food is light, flavoursome and sometimes spicey. The Hwa Li is a very popular lunch spot situated right in the centre of a large commerical building, it is split into two sections, one for general dining and the second for groups who enjoy the round 12 place dining table and the privacy of their own dining area. The menu is specialised and prepared daily by owner Chef C. Chen. Only the freshest vegetables are lightly cooked with chicken, fish, seafood, beef or pork in wonderful sauces, some more traditional, others hot and sour or spicey. This is a very well frequented restaurant which also operates a take away service in a separate area and caters for parties and groups. Those famous spring rolls in the lightest of pastry are a delight as are the hot soups and chow mien.

Hwa Li Restaurant, Tel: 45986/46534. Open: Mondays - Saturdays

Return to the main traffic lights in the centre of town, turn left towards Manzini. Take the first road to the left at the next set of traffic lights and follow the signs towards the SEDCO complex.

SEDCO

SEDCO was established in 1970 to encourage small business and individual entrepreneurs. A number of small shops are leased at low rentals to skilled tenants. Peep into each shop, you will find picture framing, dress making, tapestry, pottery and upholstery. Shop 16 is full of wedding dresses and intricate brocade outfits. Next door the tailor makes simple clothes and uniforms and undertakes repairs.

Return to the main Mbabane/Manzini road and travel towards the Ezulwini Valley. 2kms on the left hand side of the road is a turning to the Mountain Inn.

HWA LI RESTAURANT
Specialising in Chinese dishes
Dhlan'ubeka House, Mbabane
Telephone 45986, 46534
Closed Sunday

A warm personal welcome awaits you at the
Mountain Inn from your hosts,
Marc and Liz Ward.
A family run hotel.

The views from the Mountain Inn overlooking the spectacular Ezulwini Valley ("The Heavenly Place") are as magnificent as the accommodation is comfortable.
All rooms have ensuite baths, television, telephone and radio.
An excellent restaurant offers a superb a la Carte dinner and buffet luncheon.
Plus conference facilities for 120 people.
And only 1 km from the city

Tel: (09268) 42781
P.O. Box 121, Mbabane,
Swaziland
Telex 2135WD Fax 45393

THE MOUNTAIN INN

60 double rooms with ensuite bathrooms, radios, telephone and TV, coffee making machines. Conference facilities for 260 people, private boardroom, library, swimming pool and sun terrace.

The Mountain Inn is an independent hotel owned and personally run by Marc, Liz and Kevin Ward. The Hotel faces the distant Lebombo mountains and a spectacular valley surrounded by peaks which disappear into the horizon. A friendly, relaxed ambience behind which there is quiet efficiency to ensure the smooth running of both hotel and conference facilties; this is the hallmark of the Mountain Inn. A large swimming pool overlooking the spectacular view is a relaxing area for visitors and conference guests. The Friar Tuck restaurant is a lively venue offering full a la carte choices to suit families, couples and business residents and non-residents. This beautifully refurbished hotel is a great favourite with business guests and international tourists, its proximity to Mbabane is an attraction and the personal efficiency and attention to detail makes it a joy to stay in and return to again and again.

View from the Mountain Inn terrace

The Mountain Inn, P.O Box 223, Mbabane ,Tel: 42781/42799/42773 Fax: 45393

Reception at the Mountain Inn

The Mountain Inn library

A charming thatched roof country hotel set in scenic surroundings but near the capital

THE RED FEATHER RESTAURANT
A la Carte Restaurent open to non-residents. Try our saddle of lamb and other specialitities.

P.O. Box 121,
Mbabane
Swaziland
Telephone
(+268) 42235,
43208, 43184.
Fax (+268) 46465

Travel further down the Malagwane Hill past the Swazi Inn towards the Ezulwini Valley.

THE SWAZI INN

42 Bedrooms including 6 suites with ensuite bathrooms, telephones, radios and TV, coffee machines, swimming pool, Conference facilities for 170.

Located within its own highland estate, the thatched roof and cottage style architecture indicate the secluded air of this hotel which is situated so close.to the Capital. The Swazi Inn is part of a group of hotels, resorts and motels which offer hospitality to the visitor. Comfortable seating, ethnic wall hangings and a quiet country air welcome the business traveller from a busy day in town. The Swazi Inn is a popular hotel for conferences, business meetings and group get togethers. Just 6 kms form the Casino at the Royal Swazi Sun Hotel and only 2kms from Mbabane, the Swazi Inn is an excellent choice for the visitor seeking tranquil surroundings. There is a small Swazi craft hut situated outside the hotel which displays wooden carvings, sisal baskets, soapstone figures and colourful Swazi shirts.

The Swazi Inn, P.O. Box 121, Mbabane. Tel: 42235/6, Telex: 3033 WD, Fax: 46465

Entrance to the Swazi Inn Photo by Fotostudio

Coffee time at the Mall, Mbabane

Chapter 3

The Journey through the Ezulwini Valley

The journey down the Malagwane Hill	72
Health and Beauty Spa.	75
Sun International Hotels	77,78,80
Independent Hotels	72,80,86,88
Handicraft Centres	83,84,87
Scenic routes: Tea Road	74
Restaurants	73,81,86,88
Caravan Park & Resorts	73,83
Mlilwane Wildlife Sanctuary	89
Contribution by Ted Reilly	91∆17

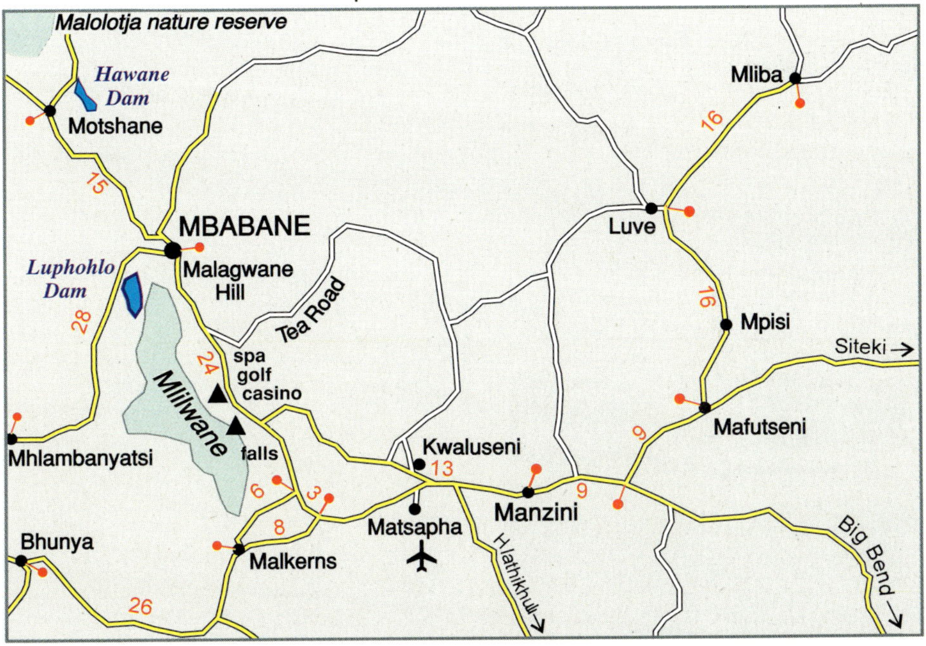

THE JOURNEY THROUGH THE EZULWINI VALLEY

The route down the Ezulwini Valley is scenically beautiful and passes the major tourist attractions within the Kingdom. As you travel down the Malagwane Hill, take exceptional care of oncoming traffic, cattle and goats. The route is steep, narrow in places and low speeds are essential. Defensive driving and awareness of others on the road will contribute to the enjoyment of this spectacular journey. Be sure to wear your seat belt at all times and to observe the 80kph speed limit and 60kph where indicated. Enjoy the steep escarpment, rolling hills, lush vegetation and distant mountain ranges which appear on both sides of the route towards the "Valley of Heaven". You are now entering the Middleveld where the temperature is slightly warmer and the vegetation more tropical.

The Ezulwini valley has long been established as the playground of the Kingdom. Along both sides of the route, you will pass handicraft centres, curio sellers, an international casino, hotels, caravan park, resorts, first class restaurants, health and beauty studios, stables, night clubs and the continuing scenic beauty of the Kingdom. All of these attractions make up the fabric of Swaziland in which the Swazi people are the cohesive thread intent on making your visit as enjoyable as possible.

During 1995 the Malagwane Hill is to be made into a major highway with four lanes of traffic, this will cause some inconvenience to travellers, but good diversions are being constructed and in the long term the road will be far safer, wider and an easier access to the the hotels, resorts and attractions in the Valley.

MGENULE MOTEL & TANDOORI RESTAURANT

30 ensuite bedrooms, with telephone, T.V. and air conditioning. Some rooms are offered on a self catering basis. Swimming pool, bar and restaurant serving Halal dishes. Travel down the Malagwane hill and on the left you will see a sign pointing to Mgenule Motel. This is a series of white painted bedrooms encircling a central restaurant and bar. The facilities are good and the rates are reasonable. The Tandoori restaurant serves freshly prepared chicken, mutton, beef, prawn and vegetable curries plus the more traditional steaks, seafood and burgers. The restaurant is open 7 days a week for lunch and dinner and offers a special menu every Friday. This is a reasonably priced venue close to the Casino, the Cuddle Puddle and the Ezulwini action.

Mgenule Motel & Tandoori Restaurant, P.O. Box 711, Mbabane, Tel/Fax: 61041/2

Ezulwini Valley
Tel: (+268) 61041

MGENULE MOTEL
Comfortable rooms at affordable prices.
Close to the Casino and Cuddle Puddle
TANDOORI RESTAURANT
The Best Indian Restaurant in Swaziland

TIMBALI CARAVAN PARK

10 kms south of Mbabane
Self-catering rooms available
Campers Welcome

P.O. Box 1, Ezulwini
Telephone: (09268) 61156

TIMBALI CARAVAN PARK

Located within 4 acres of grassed and terraced sites, Timbali Caravan Park is only 10kms from Mbabane and 2kms from the Casino. This very beautiful treed setting beneath the Mdzimba mountains has a number of amenities to ensure a carefree and happy holiday. Caravan owners, camper and chalet guests are welcome to enjoy the swimming pool, scenic walks and peace of the surroundings. In addition, self-catering rondavels and cottages are a very popular choice, these are serviced daily and are equipped with stoves, refrigerators and bedding. Remember to bring your own towels. Cooking and eating utensils are available upon request. The chalets sleep two, four or eight persons and are well placed for the centrally situated showers, baths and toilets, a general store and nearby Post Office. Timbali is a very special place, well documented in Caravanning magazines, close to the beauty of the Mdzimba mountains, the lure of the Ezulwini Valley yet not far from the business and commercial centre of Mbabane. An inexpensive place to stay where the visitor is free to come and go at leisure.

Timbali Caravan Park. P.O. Box 1, Ezulwini Tel: 61156

THE CALABASH CONTINENTAL RESTAURANT

Located immediately next to the Timbali Caravan Park is a superb restaurant known as "The Calabash Continental Restaurant", which specialises in Austrian, German and Swiss cuisine. Your host, Egon Hernler personally checks his very extensive menu to ensure that the high quality is consistently maintained. This is a highly professionally run restaurant where the choice of dishes, selection of wines, close attention to every minute detail and the discreet yet luxurious furnishings all blend to make each visit a memorable and truly enjoyable experience. The Calabash Restaurant is considered to be one of the top restaurants in the Southern African region; a select establishment with class, comfort and flair. Many residents book parties and group events at this restaurant and of course it is an excellent choice for confidential business lunches. The separate antrium bar has been designed for private meetings and small group get togethers as it is apart from the main restaurant. This is also a great venue for cocktails or after dinner Irish coffee, liquers and speciality drinks before moving onto the Casino and other late night spots. The Calabash is one of the most popular restaurants in the Kingdom, it is advisable to book a table in advance as this elegant and discreet venue is full most days. Now open 7 days a week, The Calabash is not to be missed - a superb restaurant.

The Calabash Continental Restaurant. Tel & Fax: 61187.

CALABASH CONTINENTAL RESTAURANT

Elegantly designed and furnished.
Specialists in Austrian, German and Swiss Cuisine.
Open every day for lunch and dinner.
Fully licensed.

1 km before Royal Swazi Sun Hotel & Casino

Your Host Egon
Tel/Fax: (268) 61187

A TOUCH OF BLACK FOREST
IN SWAZILAND

Return to the main Mbabane/Manzini road and immediately opposite, stop for a while at the Thandabantu Handicraft Centre. A series of individual stalls displaying hand-made basketware woven into mats, hats, carriers and ornaments, clay and wooden carvings is well sited for the passing motorist. Peep into each stall and browse around some very reasonably priced curios.

THE TEA ROAD

On the left side of the road, 10 kms from Mbabane and just before the turn off to Timbali Caravan Park and the Calabash Restaurant is a scenic route known as the Tea Road. Tea used to be grown on these hills and the road will take you above the valley overlooking the Royal area of Lobamba and across to the Mdzimba Mountain Range. The scenery is spectacular but the road is gravel, very steep in places and slippery during the summer months. Visitors are strongly advised to stay in their cars and to travel the entire road which leads back to the main Mbabane/Manzini road just 8 kms from Manzini.

The tortuous Malagwane Hill

SWAZI SPA
HEALTH & BEAUTY STUDIO

* Cuddle Puddle
* Massage
* Sauna & Spa Bath
* Under-water Massage
* Whirl & Bubble Bath (Jacuzzi)
* Fitness Centre
* Oxygen Multi-step Therapy
* Aromatherapy -steam

Situated near the Casino
Ladies & Gentlemen Welcome
Open Daily: 10am-6pm
Phone & Fax: 61164
Yours sincerely

Horst Saylor

SWAZI SPA HEALTH AND BEAUTY STUDIO

Travel a further kilometre along the valley and you come upon the Swazi Spa Health and Beauty Studio. This is a complete tonic after a long and tedious journey. Highly qualified staff under the expert eye of Horst Sayler, offer complete massage and relaxation programmes. The Swazi Spa is romantically known as the "Cuddle Puddle", where natural mineral waters flow continuously into a large swimming pool. Enjoy a professional masssage which includes the use of a machine to improve the circulation and stimulate the blood flow then the warmth and therapeutic properties of natural springs whilst undergoing an underwater massage. For the more energetic, there is a fully equipped gymnasium and keep fit area, which can be followed by a sauna and revitalising whirl and bubblebath. This whirlpool (Jacuzzl) must be the most enjoyable of treatments, thousands of bubbles like champagne gently pound the skin encouraging circulation, improving muscle hardness and gently contouring the body, this is really a great experience. A well placed aerobics area with continuous professional videos is a further feature plus the aromatherapy tube which is a steam bath with softly smelling oils which penetrate the skin. A further totally rejuvenatiing treatment is the Oxygen Multi-step Therapy which involves a short series of oxygen intakes to bring back energy and youth to your step, what a wonderful treatment to have when away from everyday cares, couple this with Aromatherapy and a totally new you emerges from the Studio ready to tackle the world!! Horst Saylor is very well versed in health matters, he offers a course of treatment together with the Oxygen Multi-step Therapy which can allay the early stages of cancer. For many young, middle aged to older people, this is a very wise treament to undertake which can easily be fitted in whilst on holiday.

Swazi Health and Beauty Studio, P. O. Box 1455, Mbabane. Tel & Fax: 61164.

ROYAL SWAZI SUN HOTEL AND CASINO HOTEL

122 Double rooms, 14 family rooms, 9 luxury suites, 18 hole golf course, Casini and slot machines, Conference Centre with 600 seat auditorium, 700 seat banqueting hall. Newly refurbished, The Royal Swazi Sun Hotel is the most luxurious Hotel in the Kingdom.

Only 1/2 km away the traveller enters the world of Sun International. The Royal Swazi Sun Hotel is located deep within the Valley of Heaven and nestles beneath the Mdzimba peaks. This is a luxury hotel which offers everything to the holiday maker, sports enthusiast or business visitor seeking luxury and efficiency in magnificent surroundings. The Royal Swazi Sun is the flagship of the Sun group within the Kingdom. Each of its 122 double, 14 family rooms and 9 suites are luxuriously furnished and tastefully decorated in discreet style. Facilities include: Planters and the Terrace Restaurants; Gigi's a la Carte Restaurant with resident band and cabaret; a poolside terrace and bar facing magnificent mountain views. The Planter's Bar and Restaurant and the Casino Bar cater for guests and visitors to the hotel. The Casino includes roulette tables, black jack and punto banco plus a large choice of slot machines.

The sports enthusiast may play on a superb 18 hole golf course, enjoy tennis under floodlights, challenge at squash in one of two courts or bowl on one of the immaculate bowling greens. Horse riding can be arranged from a local riding stable and swimming in the large terrace pool or just lazing in the sun are part of the Sun experience. An in-house cinema showing popular and adult films is located inside the Casino and television and a video channel programme are available in all rooms. Each room has a splendid view of the mountains and rolling valleys.

The Papaya and Katinka boutiques in the hotel offer the best of Swazi handicraft and imported fashions, plus those essential items you forgot to pack. There is a Barclays Bank agency for all your traveller cheques and credit card transactions. The Royal Swazi Sun is a complete holiday area in itself, enjoy an intimate dinner at "Gigi's", have a flutter on the roulette table, experience the beauty of the hotel grounds and surrounding majestic scenery, play a hard game of tennis or simply sip a long drink by the pool This is the Swaziland experience to which international visitors return time and again. The architecture, ambience, location and polite service reflect the very best of Swaziland's culture within a sophisticated environment.

Royal Swazi Sun Hotel
Private Bag, Ezulwini,
Tel: 61001, Telex: 2014WD
& 2275, Fax: 61606/61128.

Entrance to the Royal Swazi Sun Hotel. Photo by Fotostudio

Entrance to the new Casino at the Royal Swazi Sun Hotel. Photo by Fotostudio

UMHLANGA TOURS & SAFARIS

The Umhlanga Tours Team. Photo by Fotostudio

Within the Royal Swazi Sun Hotel, Swaziland's oldest established tour company, Umhlanga Tours have an office from where tours from half a day to as long as required may be booked. Umhlanga Tours operators have an intimate knowledge of the Swazi Kingdom, her traditions, culture and the African bush which are personally shown to the visitor. Within a short span of time, Umhlanga Tours will guide you through a variety of scenery ranging from the Highveld in the West to the Eastern bushveld with its African magic; truly a photographic paradise. Umhlanga Tours specialise in half, full day and overnight safaris in Swaziland's Nature Reserves and Game Sanctuaries. Game drives to Mlilwane and Mkhaya Nature Reserves to view the game and birdlife are a wonderful experience as in both reserves they can be viewed at very close quarters. The rare Black Rhino, rapidly dying out in the rest of Africa, is a frequent sighting at Mkhaya as is the growing herd of elephant who roam close to the landrover slowly touring in the park. Let Umhlanga Tours show you this "Jewel" of Africa and places beyond Swaziland's borders.

Umhlanga Tours & Safaris, P. O. Box 2197, Mbabane, Tel: 44522/61001, Fax: 42485

THE LUGOGO SUN HOTEL

202 Re-furbished and air conditioned rooms with private bathroom, telephone, radio, TV, M Net and video channel, swimming pool, Swazi Village.
Located next to the Royal Swazi Sun is the Lugogo Sun, which has the largest number of rooms in the Kingdom. There is a large terrace to cater for sporting groups, outside parties and a picnic setting "Under the Trees", which is ideal for barbeques, luncheons, traditional dancing and anniversary functions. A bus regularly travels between the Lugogo Sun, the Ezulwini Sun and the Royal Swazi Sun to enable guests to explore and use the Sun facilities at all three venues. Guests may use the Casino facilities at the Royal Swazi Sun; business visitors utilise the Convention Centre and then return to the informality of the Lugogo Sun. This is a fun hotel, where theme evenings, special events and competitions regularly take place. Every Sunday is Family Day at the Ilanga Restaurant which caters for guests and visitors to a varied buffet suiting every taste, a visiting musical group frequently entertains. Country and Western, German, Italian, Greek, French and South African evenings form part of the Lugogo experience which is very popular with visitors and local residents.

The Lugogo Sun, Private Bag, Ezulwini, Tel: 61101, Telex: 2058 WD, Fax: 61111

The Golf Course at the Royal Swazi Sun Hotel

THE EZULWINI SUN HOTEL

120 air-conditioned rooms with en suite bathrooms, telephone, TV and Video channel, radio, hairdryers, coffee shop/restaurant and swimming pool.

Opposite the Lugogo Sun is the Ezulwini Sun, which lies beneath the Lobamba and Mdzimba Mountains. Views from all of the hotel rooms are spectacular, across the pool terrace, gardens and down into the valley which becomes the Royal area of Lobamba. The Ezulwini Sun has recently altered its character and now offers the business visitor a great deal in price, facilities and friendliness. Very competitively priced, the Ezulwini has maintained an excellent standard at a very budget rate. The Coffee Shop and Restaurant serves good, wholesome dishes throughout the day until 10.30 pm plus of course the opportunity to choose from a varied a la carte menu. The Ezulwini has two all weather tennis courts and an adjoining horse-riding stable. All three Sun International hotels operate a bus to Matsapha Airport, 23 minutes away. The Lugogo and Ezulwini have their own shop and boutiques plus a pharmacy to cater for immediate needs.

The Ezulwini Sun, Private Bag, Ezulwini , Tel: 61201, Telex: 2147 WD, Fax: 61782.

Terrace and pool at the Ezulwini Sun

Restaurant at the Ezulwini Sun Hotel. Photo by Fotostudio

THE YEN SAAN HOTEL

34 air conditioned ensuite-rooms , telephone, radio and TV. Conference facilities, roof garden, swimming pool.

On the opposite side and down the road stands the Yen Saan Hotel and Chinese Restaurant. This oriental style hotel set well back from the road in spacious grounds is just 12 kms from Mbabane. Constructed from Chinese design, the Yen Saan is a comfortable hotel attracting both touring and business visitors. Chinese cuisine is a speciality of the house and its proximity to the excitement and beauty of the valley make this a favourite

YEN SAAN
HOTEL & CHINESE RESTAURANT

Luxury accommodation, all private bathrooms.
Tennis Court and Swimming Pool.
Lunch from 12 noon - 2.30 pm.
Dinner from 6.30 pm - 10.30 pm.

EZULWINI VALLEY. P.O. BOX 771, MBABANE,
KINGDOM OF SWAZILAND
TEL.& FAX (+268) 61051/2

meeting and resting place in Swaziland. Visitors can swim, play tennis, enjoy horse riding from local stables and then savour an oriental dinner with an Eastern ambience. Try this welcoming hotel where the food is always good and the company friendly.

Yen Saan Hotel, P.O. Box 771, Mbabane, Tel & Fax: 61051.

FIRST HORSE RESTAURANT

In front and to the left of the Yen Saan Hotel on your journey along the Ezulwini Valley towards Manzini is the First Horse Restaurant. A top class restaurant with a Continental flair and Eastern flavour. The First Horse, named after an Indian mounted regiment, has a varied menu including some excellent, flavoursome curries. The well stocked and welcoming bar is the first port of call for cocktails, aperitifs, or a quiet beer and for after dinner speciality coffee. Swiss owner and chef Rudi presents daily special dishes to complement the extensive a la carte range; seafood, fish, steaks, chicken dishes and some superb desserts. Always make a table booking at the First Horse and be prepared for first class cuisine, some excellent wines and attentive service.

First Horse Restaurant. Tel: 61137.

1st Horse Restaurant

Where East meets West
Enjoy delicately spiced curries
or unique continental cuisine

For reservations

☎ **61137**

Ezulwini Valley Swaziland

Gardens & swimming pool at the Yen Saan Hotel

Part of the Armstrong range

ARMSTRONG ARTWORKS

Armstrong Artworks established in 1985, is a quality screen printing workshop owned by Peter and Aleta Armstrong, which produces the African Fantasy range. It is equally well known by businesses in the Southern African region as a friendly and efficient place they can approach for all promotional items like; T-shirts, plaques, stickers, football jerseys, ceramics, logos, labels, emahiyas etc. You name it, they design and make it. Their fun T-shirts depicting Pudding the Cat and his animal friends are a delight and well known within the Kingdom. One new T-shirt design depicts the Fat Cats who always come out on top, another shows the least endangered species "The Cockcroach". In house pottery, screen printed table napkins, personalised anoraks and sweat shirts plus bumper stickers and special events screen printing are just some of the products from the Armstrong stable. For tourists wishing to view the workshop, bookings can be made with Umhlanga Tours or by appointment only. Open 8 - 5 for business and export orders. .

Armstrong Artworks, P.O. Box 291, Ezulwini, Tel: 61193, Fax: 61877

SMOKEY MOUNTAIN VILLAGE

18 Self contained chalets sleeping 3, 4 and 6 persons. Swimming pool, kiddies pool, cosy pub, small restaurant, "Usual Place" pub.

Continue on your journey for a further 2.5 kms, turn left into Smokey Mountain Village This resort contains 18 "A" framed chalets constructed in pine, each with its own verandah and braai area. This tranquil resort is wonderful for families seeking self-catering facilities, freedom, reasonable accommodation and close proximity to the vibrancy of the Valley. Each chalet is fully equipped, however, not all are air-conditioned. There is a swimming pool and intimate restaurant for residents and visitors. Smokey Mountain Village has its own cosy "The Usual Place" bar, which is a favourite watering place for many local residents and visitors. Wednesdays are darts and pool nights at "Smokies" when you can meet local residents, have a super game of darts, bar snacks and perhaps win a small prize.

Smokey Mountain Village, P.O. Box 21, Ezulwini Tel: 61291/61293, Fax: 46465

* Chalet Motel
* Asihlangane Restaurant
* Darts every Wednesday
* Soft Music & Pool Table

Reasonable Accommodation

P.O. Box 21, Ezulwini, Swaziland. Tel (+268) 61291, 61293 Fax (+268) 46465

From the Smokey Mountain Village, turn right onto the tarred road which runs parallel with the main road. You are now entering the handicraft area of the Ezulwini Valley.

MANTENGA CRAFT CENTRE

Travel 1/2 km and turn right to Mantenga Craft, identified by one or two carvings of fairytale animals, where there is a series of sales outlets and a showroom of crafts which form part of the Mantenga Foundation. Founded in 1974, the Mantenga Craft Village has concentrated on long term training to encourage Swazi crafts and income generating activities. The emphasis is upon self employment especially among women and the disadvantaged. Crafts are identified for their excellence and encouraged as commercially viable ventures. The Mantenga Craft Centre markets the finished goods and pays a fair price to promote self sufficiency. The Centre also includes a number of private enterprise operations where crafts are manufactured and sold. The best of Swazi crafts are here from individually designed T-shirts, jewellery, mohair tapestries and clothing, hand woven table cloths, material, bedspreads, handmade toys, soap-stone, clay and wooden carvings to intricate basketware. A workshop for training in artisitic practicality forms one of the areas in the corridor of shops. Here hand painted flower and plant pots, children's laquered furniture and other creative skills are experimented and taught. Mantenga Craft Centre has blossomed and grown in the past year, the selection of crafts is greater and the number of new craft enterprises has increased. All this is good for Mantenga as a nurturing and marketing centre and for the visitor wishing to view the variety and quality of Swazi Crafts. The series of small shops encompass, hand woven wool rugs, gold and silver locally designed and manufactured jewellery, pine furniture made by the handicapped. handmade leatherware, painted ostrich eggs, handwoven crochet and the creative work at African Fantasy retailed from the Mantenga Craft Centre,
Mantenga Craft Centre, P.O Box A5, Swazi Plaza, Mbabane. Tel: 61136, Fax: 61040

AFRICAN FANTASY AT MANTENGA

*African Fantasy at Mantenga
Photo by Fotostudio*

Aleta Armstrong runs her African Fantasy shop at Mantenga Craft Centre, which incorporates all of the artistry and practiical manufacture of the Armstrong range. The recognizeable "Pudding the Cat" label which is the copyright of this collection includes T-shirts and sweat shirts with a conservation bias. . Come and see the traditional Wild African Cats and African Nights designs plus many others. Colour in posters, cards and children's pencil boxes, fun stickers, table mats and mugs all form part of the magic of this shop. Embedded in the wall is the front of a VW Kombi carrying passengers Kermit and Miss Piggy without seatbelts after a road accident - an evergreen topical subject. Come and see, enjoy, browse while the children colour in cards and you have time to ponder.
African Fantasy at Mantenga, P.O. Box 291, Ezulwini. Tel: 61136, Fax: 61178.

Mantenga Craft CENTRE

Woven, cotton, wool, rugs, tablecloths, tapestries, pottery, ornamentalware, ceramics, sculptures, vases, ovenware, silkscreen and blockprint cotton, sarongs, mahiyas, tablecloths, posters, cards, tee-shirts, silverware, jewellery, earrings, necklaces, bracelets, rings, skirts, dresses, cushion covers, tea towels, Leather bags and shoes, crochet work.

REPRESENTED

AFRICAN FANTASY
RUDI'S RUGS
LITTLE SILVER SHOP
PINE CORNER
FLUID DESIGN
GONE RURAL
SWAZI CROCHET CENTRE

AFRICAN IMPRESSIONS
ROSECRAFT
IMBUTI TAPESTRIES
BAOBAB BATIK
NGWENYA GLASS
LUBO'S SHOP
SOUTHERN COMFORT

Open daily from 8.00 am
P.O. Box A5, Swazi Plaza, Mbabane, Kingdom of Swaziland
Tel: (+268) 61136 Fax: (+268) 61040

The Little Silver Shop

ORIGINAL GOLD & SILVER JEWELLERY, ETHNIC BEADS, MODERN AND FUN DESIGNS, PLUS GIFTS FOR THE HOME

Open 7 days a week
**At Mantenga Craft Centre
Tel: 61136, Fax: 61040**

LITTLE SILVER SHOP

Within the series of shops is a jewellery outlet which specialises in gold and silver locally manufactured pieces by "Gold and Silver". Delicate earrings, chains, rings, pendants and much more is designed and made in the Mantenga area. Qualified goldsmiths have received years of practical training and can make any jewellery item in gold or silver in a selection of simple or intricate designs. The choice is wide to suit specific tastes. This is the shop to visit for light gifts to take home or for something specifically made to your own design. Elephant hair bracelets in gold and silver, also charms of rhino, warthogs and elephant. Diamond studs earrings can be found and rings are fabricated in precious and semi precious stones; the range includes wedding bands and sets. All of these are made in this creative part of Swaziland and can be purchased from the Little Silver Shop.

Little Silver Shop, P.O. Box A75, Swazi Plaza, Mbabane. Tel: 61136, Fax: 61040

THE MANTENGA FALLS HOTEL

18 ensuite luxury double rooms, T.V. swimming pool, sauna, trampoline, a la carte restaurant. Travel past the road to the Mantenga Falls and stop at the Mantenga Lodge. This newly renovated hotel is set within a very beautiful area, tall riverine trees overhang the terrace, gardens and sparkling pool. All bedrooms have been refurbished and the view across to the Nyonyane peak and the valleys beneath is wonderful. There is a very intimate bar at the Mantenga Lodge, just the place to meet other guests and enjoy the personal attention of the owners and their staff. In summer the outside terrace is a magical place to sit and enjoy a sundowner. Next to the quaint bar is the a la carte restaurant, well furnished and served with top class dishes prepared by the professional chef. The Mantenga Lodge is a new venue within Swaziland where families can relax and couples enjoy the tranquillity and beauty of the Mantenga area.

**Mantenga Lodge, P.O. Box 68, Ezulwini
Tel & Fax: 61049**

Mantenga Lodge

Charming Country Hotel offering luxury accommodation.
Swimming Pool, Sauna, trampoline.
A la Carte Restaurant and bar.
Close to Casino, Golf Course and Nature Reserve.

**Box 68, Ezulwini
Kingdom of Swaziland
Tel / Fax: (268) 61049**

Happy Valley Motel

Unique!!!

Motel with the Difference

Quiet and secluded bedrooms away from the entertainment complex.
All rooms with two double beds, air conditioning, telephone, fridge, and Satellite TV.

Sir Loin Steakhouse
Open Monday to Saturday
7.00 pm till late

Vienna Coffee Shop
Open 6.30 am - midnight
Continental Cakes.
Full range of delicious quick meals.

Why Not Disco Night Club

Cabaret
11.45 pm and 1.30 pm Nightly.

If Not Go-Go Bar
Open 7.00 pm
Non-stop action

Mbabane/Manzini Road
PO Box 5, Ezulwini,
Kingdom of Swaziland
Tel: (+268) 61061/61199
Fax: (+268) 61050

HAPPY VALLEY MOTEL

57 Rooms with ensuite bath, TV with 2 video channels in all rooms, coffee making machines, fridge, telephone, secure parking outside rooms, swimming pool, nightclub and discotheque, restaurant, coffee shop, pool room and bars.

The last hotel within the Ezulwini Valley is the Happy Valley Motel. This is a Mecca of Entertainment, a vibrant, swinging venue for those seeking evening entertainment. Not only a night spot, the Happy Valley Motel has a swimming pool for those leisurely summer days. In the old Continental tradition, the Vienna Coffee Shop offers a leisurely breakfast plus a selection of imported magazines and BBC TV is now an early morning feature in the Vienna Coffee Shop which stays open from 6.30 - 12.00 midnight.

At night, the Happy Valley changes from a relaxed and quiet venue to a hot spot of Swaziland's night life. Latest International shows, artists and entertainers and music play in the "Why Not Disco Night Club", up to the minute discos and continuous video films make this a popular venue for visitors. Visit the Sirloin Steakhouse which opens each night until very late, except Sunday, for hungry dancers, sportsmen and diners. The Poolroom and bar is a popular spot for English pub visitors and the Lions Den Sports Bar plays action sports direct from M-Net or satellite. The Happy Valley Motel has a stimulating atmosphere for the young at heart seeking exciting and different entertainment. From a game of pool to topical International sport beamed by satelite TV in the Lions Den bar, supper in the Sir-Loin Steakhouse and late night fun in the "If Not, Why Not" Go Go Bar and the Why Not, this is a resort to be experienced, to enjoy adult entertainment and to have a great deal of fun.

The Happy Valley Motel P.O. Box 5, Ezulwini. Tel: 61061/61199/61898, Fax: 61050

Somersault and friends at Mlilwane Wildlife Sanctuary

Horse riders at Mlilwane on a guided horse trail. Photo by Big Game Parks

MLILWANE WILDLIFE SANCTUARY

No visit to the Ezulwini Valley is complete without entering the Mlilwane Wildlife Sanctuary which covers 4,500 hectares. This secluded and incredibly beautiful sanctuary is only 4 kms from the Casino yet contains a great variety of mammals, birds, trees and plants. Set in a bowl beneath the Mdzimba mountain range in which the Swazi Royal ancestors are buried, Mlilwane is a haven of tranquillity. Enjoy the unspoilt peace of this very accessible reserve where you will see graceful giraffe, skittish zebra, shy wildebeest, numerous impala, nyala and the everpresent warthog.

The background to Mlilwane is both depressing and inspiring. In the 1940's, the Valley of Heaven was teaming with game, birds, and tall grass. By the mid 1950's almost all of the wildlife had disappeared due partly to hunting and to displacement as a result of modern farming and industrial techniques. Several efforts to solicit financial support from government proved unsuccessful Eventually, Swaziland's renowned conservationist, Ted Reilly and his family decided to change the character of their private family farming estate and to create a sanctuary using their own private means. Creation of suitable habitats in which game would flourish was a formidable task. Slowly, Mlilwane was filled with varying species of game. These were caught one by one, darted, placed in an ageing Landrover and transported to Mlilwane. From these worrying, tense yet determined early days, Mlilwane has become a growing sanctuary and haven for the re-introduction of vanishing breeds.

In the early 1960's the rest camp was constructed and opened to the public, this is

Blue Crane in the Camp

now a very popular area for visitors. Thatched huts arranged around a central hippo pool, together with traditional beehive huts and a timberlog cabin dormitory and a recently-built self contained cottage form the overnight accommodation. You can also bring your own caravan or tent and camp overnight.

From the early day of single species, gifts from Natal Parks of giraffe, white rhino, warthog, nyala and hippo have now developed into herds of game, large enough to donate to Hlane, Mkhaya, Malolotja and Mlawula. But the struggle against poaching continues, witnessed by the large collection of snares displayed as you enter Mlilwane.

Mlilwane has a large area of open grasslands so game viewing is easy. Visitors who have a short time in the Kingdom have the opportunity to spot a large variety of mammals and birds in limited time. Drive slowly across the dam and watch for signs of crocodile, Egyptian geese and shy waterbuck. The pool located within the centre of the rest camp houses hippo, crocodile and blue cranes, plus a great variety of birdlife. Carefully watch for movement from the "Hippo Haunt", which is a restaurant overlooking the pool. You will spot turtles swimming so close that you can almost touch them, hippos raising their heads to be photographed, and crocodiles slithering from the bank to the water. A truly unique sight is feeding time at 3:00pm every day at the rest camp, when hippos, birds and warthog compete for the birdfood. This occurs within 3 metres of the visitor, who is protected by a 1 metre high stone wall. A large heronry of nesting egrets, herons and ibis occupy an island in the hippo pool. Visitors may buy provisions from the camp shop or arrange to eat in the "Hippo Haunt' from an unusual menu including warthog, impala and venison. Alternatively, you may watch your dinner being roasted over an open fire while you enjoy the night sounds. Take your own braai and cook over individual fires, savour the different smells and enjoy the atmosphere of Mlilwane after dark. A night pass may be obtained from the camp and visitors can visit the Casino and luxury hotels within the valley and then return to the natural unspoilt environment of Mlilwane.

Horse rides through the sanctuary taking in the superb scenery and plentiful game is another Mlilwane experience. Self-guided mountain trails through the remote areas of the reserve is a wonderful way to commune with Africa, experiencing the smell, heat, and excitement of close encounters with wildlife. Umhlanga Tours run morning

and afternoon tours within the reserve or book overnight accommodation and special braai get togethers for small and larger groups. A large swimming pool is a feature of the camp where poolside braais in the hot weather are a popular choice.
Amazingly, all of this natural experience is present just a few kms from Mbabane. The close proximity of wild Africa to the sophisticated urban life is the intriguing paradox of Swaziland. Both can be explored and enjoyed without travelling for hours over hot, dusty roads. Mlilwane's greatest contribution to Swaziland is that she has precipitated the creation of all the other Parks and all that is nature conservation in the Kingdom today. Mlilwane have introduced a new mountain bike attraction enabling visitors to enjoy the reserve from the bicycle perspective. Bikes can be hired by the hour or longer from the central Rest Camp, cyclists need to be accompanied by a guide who will point out game, and the ecological variations in this very scenic sanctuary

Mlilwane Wildlife Sanctuary, P.O. Box 234, Mbabane, Tel: 44541, Fax: 40957
A/H and weekends, Tel: 61037/61591/2/3, Fax: 61594.
Central Resevations Office: Shop 16, the Mall, Mbabane.

BABY MIRACLE (Reproduced by kind permission of Ted Reilly)

The birth of a hippo might not seem a momentous event to most. But at Mlilwane Wildlife Sanctuary, the latest arrival in the famed and popular hippo pool at the camp has been met with much jubilation and surprise. The baby was born in March this year and is thriving. It is the first hippo calf ever to be born on a Reserve in Swaziland.

The new-born calf is the offspring of the only bull in the pool - Somersault - and a cow called Lucia. It has taken 13 years of having at least one bull and one cow together at a time in the pool for a baby to show its face. The question stumping the management and conservationist of Mlilwane is, "WHY?"

Live hippos are selling on open market nowadays at about E20 000 apiece. So if the herd in the pool, presently comprising 1 bull and 3 cows (without the addition of the calf) had not produced an offspring (which up until this year it appeared they would not), it would have been an expensive job ensuring the continuation of the species at Mlilwane. But fortunately, the hippos themselves solved the dilemma of what was to be done, by finally "getting their act together." This new member of the family has an interesting family history behind it.

Somersault was the very first hippo at Mlilwane, translocated from the Kruger National Park in 1979. He was joined in 1979 by his first "wife", Winnie - a female donated when she was just one year old by the London Zoological Society and making headlines in newspapers worldwide when she made her epic flight, sponsored by South African Airways, from England to Africa. Winnie dates her ancestry back to Kenya, is a product of "incest" - her father and grandfather being one and the same hippo. Both Somersault and Winnie are still living in the hippo pool at Mlilwane.

Two more females have since been introduced to the Reserve - Lucia and Mazeze. Mazeze was in fact a 21st birthday present to Mlilwane by the Natal Parks Board in 1985, and her name (the English translation of which is a "flea") came about from the observation that her back bears a striking resemblance to a flea.

So it had generally been accepted that Somersault must be sterile, as it was highly unlikely that the 3 females were all infertile. And although in all this time no baby had appeared, there had been plenty of signs of mating between Somersault and his harem. So what was to be done to propagate the species at Mlilwane?

It was known from experience that Somersault would not tolerate a competitor in the way of another female hippo in the pool. Competition had once come in, in the form of Macobane - a bull brought over by South African Airways again from Whipsnade Zoo in England. Somersault attacked him and chased him further and further afield until eventually the poor newcomer fled through a fence and right out of the Reserve. He was severely gashed and injured, but after having been pulled into a crate by a tractor and removed to Mkhaya Nature Reserve in the lowveld, he survived, and still survives today. Two females have since been introduced into Macobane's domain at Mkhaya, and the second population of protected hippo in Swaziland has now flourished there as a result of his introduction.

So the sensible thing to do appeared to be to get rid of Somersault and replace him with another, fertile, bull. Or he could have been sold as a hunting trophy to a Park in South Africa. Certainly the money would have come in useful buying another hippo. But both of these options seemed unthinkable to those who had to make the decision. Somersault is a mascot of Mlilwane. He has been there for as long as anyone can remember and is a favourite among visitors and staff alike. Somersault is probably the most photographed hippo in the wild in the world today. Photographs of him have even been used to advertise Game Parks in other countries!

So it was decided that the "sensible" thing would not be done. Hearts were allowed to rule heads, and Somersault stayed right where he was, and still is today. Perhaps this baby is Somersault's gift of gratitude and love to those who stuck so loyally by his side, even at the expected expense of forfeiting the chance of the natural propagation of the hippos at Mlilwane.

Giraffe at Mlilwane. Photo by Big Game Parks

One other possibility has been suggested for the absence of baby hippo to date. That is that other calves have been born but have all been males and, as is common among hippos, they have been killed at birth by an adult bull. However, this is a highly remote possibility, as this could not have been happening for 13 years without being noticed.

The young calf is a female named Thembi and is doted upon by Somersault. Often you will see it surfacing from under the water riding on Somersault's neck. We would love to have a clear photo of it to include here, but it appears still to be camera-shy (unlike her father) and the only way you can see it is to visit her. (Since Thembi's arrival another female calf has been born named Mazezane which means "Little Flea" after her mother - Mazeze).

Chapter 4

The Journey through Lobamba to Manzini

The Royal area of Lobamba	96
Houses of Parliament	98
Museum	98
The Malkerns Valley	99 - 102
Restaurants	106, 107
Handicraft Centres	99, 100, 101
The Hub of the Nation - Manzini	104

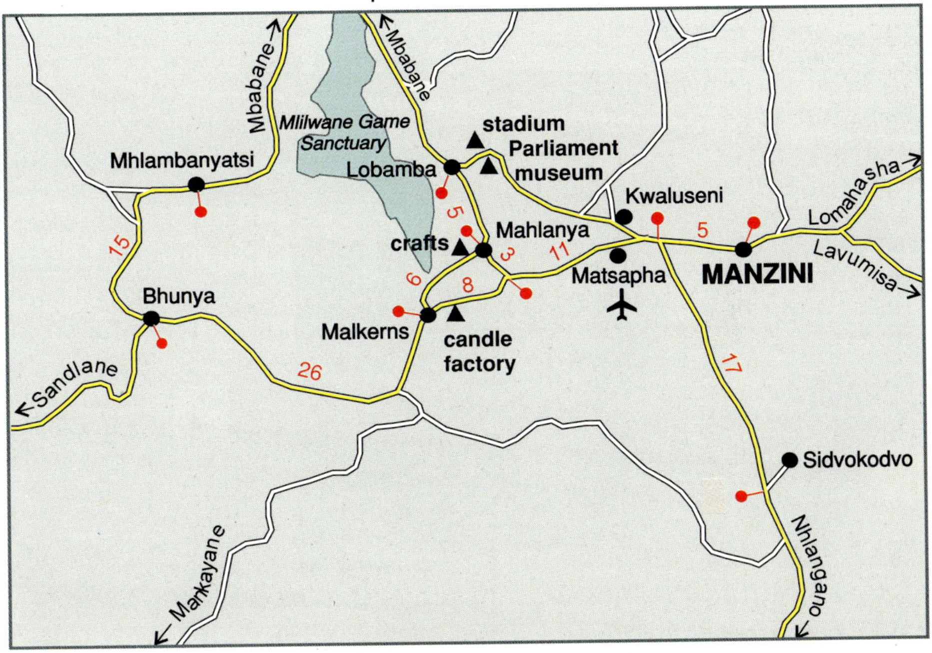

93

The Nation's Bank with the Complete Package

Because we are Swaziland's Development Bank, we understand and care...

For your basic needs:
* Agricultural Loans
* Housing Loans

For your international Transactions
* Foreign Exchange Facilities

For your development needs:
* Business Loans
* Commercial Loans

and for your personal convenience
* Savings & Current Accounts

Come and Save with us because your development is our Business

Head Office: Egungwini, Allister Miller Street, Mbabane.
P.O.Box 336, Telephone: 42551/8, Telex: 2396 WD, Fax:41214

Swaziland Development & Savings Bank

Swaziland Development and Savings Bank have opened a branch at the New Mall, Mbabane where their commercial customers will receive personal attention to all of their financial affairs. This expansion is to assist with all industrial and commercial transactions making banking easier and more accessible. A department for foreign exchange is in place for international business transactions.

Swaziland Development & Savings Bank is committed to the commercial and social prosperity of Swaziland by offering financial backing and technical assistance to enterprising individuals and companies of the Nation.

THE JOURNEY THROUGH LOBAMBA TO MANZINI

Your route now takes you to the Royal area of Lobamba, which is the centre of Government within the Kingdom. King Mswati III maintains the Royal Kraal in Lobamba in which the ritual of the Ncwala takes place in December/January each year. In addition, the Reed Dance is performed in August/September outside the Royal Kraal in the presence of His Majesty (the Ingwenyama) and the King's Mother (the Ndlovukazi). At specific times, His Majesty will summon his people to the Royal Kraal to advise them of certain issues and to listen to suggestions from the Swazi nation regarding the administration of the Kingdom. This enables all citizens to air their views on particular topics. His Majesty's Council will then convene to confer with His Majesty, and subsequently report back to the Nation. Resolutions are then formulated into legislation in the two Houses of Parliament. In October 1993, a General Election took place which has changed the political running of the country on more democratic lines.

SOMHLOLO NATIONAL STADIUM

On the left you will notice the Somhlolo National Stadium, which is used for major celebrations and events in the Kingdom. It was here that His Majesty King Mswati III celebrated with the Swazi Nation after his Coronation in April 1986. The Pope visited Swaziland in 1988 and addressed the Swazi people from the Somhlolo Stadium. In July 1989 a 21st Birthday concert was held to raise funds for the King's Trust His Majesty's 25th birthday and the Kingdom's 25th Anniversary celebrations in September 1993 were held at this stadium. In addition, the Somhlolo Stadium is frequently used for international major soccer events which are televised live on Swazi TV from their newly acquired Outside Broadcasting Unit.

King Sobhuza II Memorial at Lobamba

THE KING SOBHUZA II MEMORIAL PARK
SWAZILAND NATIONAL TRUST COMMISSION
LOBAMBA

Tours organized through Umhlanga Tours at Royal Swazi Sun Hotel

Enquiries
PO Box 100,
Lobamba
Swaziland
Tel: (268) 61178 / 9
(268) 61151
Fax: (268) 61875

HOUSES OF PARLIAMENT
Located next to the Stadium are the Houses of Parliament and the National Museum. The Houses of Parliament are open to visitors who may enter each of the chambers in the company of an official guide. The House consists of two chambers; the Upper House or Senate and the House of Assembly. The Senate has 20 members of which 10 have traditionally been selected by His Majesty and the balance by the House of Assembly. The Lower House has 50 members. In October 1993, a general election was held, the first on more democratic lines. Members of the Lower house were elected by democratic vote and the cabinet to be selected from those nominated members. Parliament is opened by His Majesty, legislation is considered, debated and passed by both Houses. Visitors may attend parliamentary debates. They will be guided to the Public Gallery to listen to debates in both official languages - English and siSwati.

NATIONAL MUSEUM
Next to the Houses of Parliament, you will find the National Museum which contains a compact and informative series of displays depicting Swazi origins, tradition, dress and lifestyle. As the visitor sees so many Swazi men dressed in traditional clothes, the meaning and background of the culture is of particular interest. During ceremonial occasions Swazi men carry shields of their regiment. Young men aged under 25 carry a multi-coloured shield of brownish red with a baboon skin tied around the stick. More mature men use black and white skin to cover their shields, adorned with a monkey skin. The elders can easily be identified by the larger grey shields, which carry the jackal's skin on the stick. Traditional dress includes the loin cloth (emahiya) worn under lion skins or pelts and the carrying of a knobkerry. Swazi women also wear a skin skirt together with a loin apron and cloak. Both men and women adorn themselves with beads, necklaces and anklets.

Next to the display cabinet are a series of old photographs portraying Swazi history together with an informative narrative. Early photographs of King Sobhuza II and the external influences which shaped part of the Swazi heritage will enlighten the visitor about the history of the Kingdom. The Museum staff are extremely helpful and well informed. A visit to the Museum helps to fill the gaps of your growing knowledge of the experience of Swaziland. Next to the Museum is a traditional Swazi Homestead consisting of four beehive huts. A guide will advise of the uses of the huts and the traditional placement of them within the homestead.

Continue past the Houses of Parliament and the road will lead to the Royal Lozitha Palace which is used for ceremonial and official occasions. Visitors may view the exterior only and the taking of photographs is prohibited..

Return to the main Mbabane-Manzini road and continue towards Manzini for a further 7 kms. You will come to a sign pointing to the right towards Mankayane, Piet Retief, Bhunya and Mhlambanyati, turn right here and only 1 km on your right, you will find Tishweshwe Crafts and Malandela's Restaurant just before the village of Malkerns. Malkerns is a well established valley as a major farming area. Its fertile soil and plentiful rainfall nurtures sugar cane, pineapples, tumeric, roses, strawberries and vegetables. Lining the valley are the pine and eucalyptus trees of the Usutu Forest. The Malkerns irrigation canal runs through the area irrigating the fruit, grain and vegetable crops.

Tishweshwe Crafts at Malkerns.

TISHWESHWE CRAFTS

Tishweshwe Crafts is a series of decorated cottages with thatched roofs and clay walls. This handicraft centre began 14 years ago when the owners encouraged local men and women in the fields of weaving, stone and wood sculpture, sewing and pottery. Individual crafts are assisted with equipment, dyes, tools and experience. Tishweshwe has grown to become a marketing and exhibition area for individual talent and handicraft. Of special interest is Lutindzi grass weaving, which is exceptionally fine work involving the collection of grasses from the mountains. These are made malleable, dyed into bright colours and plaited to make baskets, mats and floor coverings.

The shop displays crafts from all over Africa from pottery to beadwork, fine carvings and ethnic materials. Tapestries, wall hangings and rugs, are all handmade from Swaziland and the surrounding region. There is a corner containing children's books plus editions on

 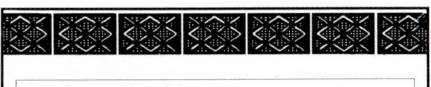

Tishweshwe Crafts

Traditional crafts from all over Africa.
Basketry, pottery, handpainted cloth, leather work from Swaziland.
Mohair rugs and tapestries.
Clothing and jewellery.
Wide range of cards and giftwrap in our book section.
Licensed Restaurant attached.
Only 10 km from Ezulwini Valley towards Manzini; turn right into Malkerns Road

Tel: 83336
Open 7 days a week

Swazican
Swaziland Fruit Canners (Pty) Ltd

PO Box 77, Malkerns,
Kingdom of Swaziland
Tel: (09268) 83001 - 5
Fax: (09268) 83235

GROWERS, PRODUCERS AND EXPORTERS OF:
* Pineapple Pieces, Slices, Juices and Concentrates.
* Citrus Fruits Canned and Concentrated Juice.
* Jams - Mixed Fruit, Apricot, Peach and Marmalades.

Factory prices to the public.
Tours by arrangement.

Southern African geography, history and politics. Plenty to browse over, enjoy and buy as a personal souvenir of the Kingdom or as presents for those you left behind. At the rear of the shop, a traditional Swazi homestead stands and a licensed restaurant is attached to Tishweshwe for morning coffee or lunch whilst considering a purchase.
Tishweshwe Crafts, P.O. Box 376, Malkerns. Tel: & Fax: 83336.

SWAZILAND FRUIT CANNERS

Continue past Tishweshwe Crafts and you come to Swazican on your right. Swaziland Fruit Canners (Pty) Ltd grow and can pineapples. In addition they buy grapefruit and oranges from Swaziland lowveld farmers and can all of their fruits for the export market. The Malkerns valley contains hectares of pineapple fields which together with the large canning and jam making factory provide employment for up to 3000 employees in the harvesting seasons. Visitors may visit the cannery on conducted tours which take place on Thursdays only from 8.00am to 1.00pm and from 2.00pm to 4.00pm. Tours must be prebooked through the Production Manager's secretary. A visit to Swazican includes watching the fruit being cored, peeled, then conveyed to the factory where it is sliced into rings or chunks. This is a very exciting part of the process; to watch hundreds of women dexterously select, slice or cut the fruit in seconds. The final step is to the laboratory where samples of fruit are rigourously checked for quality. As Swaziland's pineapples, grapefuit and oranges are exported all over the world to famous suppliers such as John West, Trouthall, Tesco, Safeway and Libby's, quality control is of prime importance, Visitors may like to know that no part of the fruit is wasted. Juice is canned and the peel and core of the fruit is dried and made into animal feed pellets. Telephone Swaziland 83001 for a Thursday tour.

Your journey takes you through the village of Malkerns, past the Police Station and to the Junction. Turn left towards Manzini and you will see Swazi Candles signposted to the right about 1km along this road.

SWAZI CANDLES

Swazi Candles are situated in a farmhouse environment where Swazi craftsmen and women mould each candle to its unique and individual shape.Unique to Africa, Swazi Candles began as a very clever idea which has mushroomed into a thriving cottage industry. The outer shells are designed and manufactured then cut into manageable sizes and fashioned into shape by hand. Each vibrant colour is slowly

SWAZI CANDLES

moulded over the inner white wax and gradually the shape and look of each candle comes alive in the hands of skilled craftsmen. The visitor may watch the entire process from the gentle softening of the two waxes, the deliberate moulding of each candle to the final trimming. The choice is wide and each candlemaker copies form and shape from photos then instils his own character into the individual piece; amused bulls, sad tortoise, rather severe elephants and happy hippo, the range of expressions is wide and varied. Choose from a selection of balls, mushrooms, eggs, birds, elephant, rhino, bulls and tortoises, the choice is wide and vibrant. Take home a little part of Swaziland. Colourful, warm and alive, Swazi Candles are an apt souvenir of this beautiful Kingdom and her friendly, happy people. Just to enjoy the music and atmosphere of Swazi Candles is an experience in itself.

Swazi Candles, P.O. Box 172, Malkerns. Tel: 83219, Fax: 83135

BAOBAB BATIK

Cards, wallhangings, cushion covers, clothing for children and adults.

P.O. Box 35, Malkerns, Swaziland
Tel/Fax (+268) 83177
Nyanza, Malkerns Valley

Turn right onto the road towards Manzini and stop at Nyanza Stables on your left. A small nursery, and farm shop is situated here. Baobab Batik have a very interesting shop at Nyanza exhibiting colourful printed clothing to stunning wall hangings, come and view, browse and buy a handmade batik in the vibrant and muted colours of Swazi craft. Batik work is a fairly long process requiring skill, artistry and great patience, each piece of material is carefully painted in wax to create the design and then dyed gradually building up a specific pattern. The range covers wall hangings, table cloths, napkins, greeting cards, childrens and adult clothes. Each design is entirely original and no two peices are identical. Batik maker Els Hooft has built a small cottage industry from an initial home craft industry, her staff learn and pass on the techniques to their home environment.

Baobab Batik, P.O. Box 35, Malkerns, Tel & Fax: 83177,

Swazi Candles. Photo by Fotostudio

Baobab Batik workshop. Photo by Fotostudio

Nyanza is one of many independent stables in the Kingdom situated in the very beautiful Malkerns Valley. The road meanders between agricultural fields and beneath surrounding mountain ranges. Continue past the Royal residence on the right where you may see a flock of ostrich or a few zebra; do not stop to take photographs as this is a private residence. At the junction, turn right and you have regained the main Mbabane to Manzini road.

SHIBA RUGS

Travel only 1 km from this turnoff and you will see Bethany Mission on your left. There is a series of small workshops within the Mission and Shiba Rugs have their handcraft workshop here. Visitors who have already visited the Mantenga Craft Centre will have seen the Shiba Rug shop with its selection of handwoven cotton rugs. These are very attractive and versatile and they are made in soft colours which are easy to wash and look good in a lounge, bedroom or bathroom. Shiba rugs are exported worldwide and are further proof of the diversity of talent, creativity and industry which is present in Swaziland.

Shiba Rugs, P.O. Box 155, Matsapha
Tel: 61136/84821, Fax: 61040

The journey from this junction to Manzini is 15 kms along a relatively straight road. Approximately 4kms on the right hand side

---

SHIBA RUGS

Exclusive Handmade Cotton Rugs.

MARKETING OUTLET
Mantenga Craft Centre
Ezulwini Valley
Tel: (268) 61136 Fax: (268) 61040

Bethany Handcraft Mission
PO Box 155,
Matsapha, Swaziland
Tel: (268) 84821

you will pass the Chinese Agricultural Mission. This is a farming experiment sponsored by the Republic of China where the cultivation of rice, fruit and grains are studied. The visitor will observe many rice paddy fields on both sides of the road. Swazi farmers are trained in the growth of these crops by resident Chinese experts.

On the left you pass "Paradise Caravan Park" a popular local venue. On the right is situated the "Salt 'N Pepper Club" for members to enjoy a relaxed meal and entertainment. Next to here on the right is "High Hope" Riding School and Stables. This stable specialises in pony camps for young people aged 5 years or more. Children may stay for 3 days for a reasonable fee which includes full board accommodation and riding lessons. Picnic rides and outrides for children and adults are very popular.

A further 2 kms bring you to the industrial area of Matsapha located right off the main road. Just before this turning is "Las Cabanas" Restaurant next to a large service station. Matsapha Industrial sites house the bulk of Swaziland's industry including Swaziland's Brewery, the Coca Cola factory, numerous engineering, agricultural and commercial concerns which employ thousands of Swazi people and underpin the rapidly expanding Swaziland economy.

CHESHIRE HOMES

Within Matsapha, turning left before Swaziland Bottling Company, is a rehabilitation centre located in a series of purpose built structures. A Physiotherapy room, workshop, showroom, occupational therapy facility and residential quarters are placed together specifically for the handicapped. Locally trained staff care for day and residential patients who make and sell cards, keyrings, jewellery and clothes in order to raise funds for the centre. Funding is local to underpin the supply of special furniture and equipment for the handicapped. Visitors may view the handcraft in the Cheshire Homes showroom and any purchase will assist in the ongoing running of this very dedicated centre.

Cheshire Homes, Tel: 86334

SWAZILAND HOSPICE AT HOME

Swaziland Hospice at Home have their headquarters at Matsapha, next to the Paradise Caravan Park on land donated to them where their administration block and newly finished day-care centre are situated. Most of Hospice work is done away from their offices within the homes of the terminally ill. The Hospice has been open for over three years and in September 1993 the day-care centre was opened by Prince

AVIS

MATSAPHA INTERNATIONAL AIRPORT

P.O. Box 31 Manzini - Swaziland
Tel: (268) 84928, 86226
Fax: (268) 86227 Tlx: 3008 WD
Depot: (268) 86350, 86222

Edward of Great Britain, a celebration which all will remember. Swaziland Hospice at Home have established themselves as a very worthy organization helping to alleviate the pain and suffering of the terminally ill and their relatives. Swaziland Hospice at Home have trained staff who travel all over the country to tend to the ill, administering pain-relieving medicines, listening, consoling and assisting in many ways to help both the patient and the immediate family. They are funded totally by voluntary donations and have in the past year managed to purchase vital medical equipment and expand their staff number to meet the needs of those in terminal pain. Visitors may like to give a donation to this very worthy cause or to contact the organizers for more information.

Swaziland Hospice at Home, P.O. Box 23, Matsapha, Tel: 84485

The final 8kms to Manzini is marked by urban development. A prominent turning to the right pointing to Matsapha Airport leads to Swaziland's airport where Scanair, Avis and Hertz have offices. A second turning to the right only 3 kms before Manzini points to Nhlangano and Hlatikulu. This is an exceptionally picturesque route to be covered later, in Chapter 5.

MANZINI

Manzini is situated in the centre of the Kingdom and is known as the "Hub" of the nation for this reason. From Manzini the main arterial roads to the south, north, east and west converge. The railway network to Maputo, Durban and Richard's Bay centres near to Manzini. At one stage in Swaziland's history, Manzini was the capital of Swaziland. Known as Bremersdorp after businessman Alfred Bremer, the town became the first white capital of Swaziland when the Provisional Government of Britain, the South African Republic and Swaziland ruled the Nation. Headquarters were based at the Bremer's Hotel where a number of adventurers, hunters and rogues congregated; tales of instant justice in the form of shootings and knifings abound when there was little overall control. This was in 1892 and Manzini recently celebrated its 100th anniversary, the first Swaziland town to achieve its centenary. The name was changed to Manzini which seems to derive from the Siswati word "emantini" or "in the water" is a very apt name for this previously troubled area. Swazis must have watched with amazement the endless argument between the British and the Boers until Manzini was sacked during the Boer War and the administrative centre was moved to Mbabane.

Modern Manzini has a fine golf course, country club and swimming pool. The Mall in central Manzini has a large selection of new shops. Built on what was the Railway headquarters in Manzini, the Mall is ideally placed for central shopping. It offers underground parking to shoppers and a wealth of new shops. The O.K. Bazaars opened their doors for the first time in Manzini and Woolworths came to Swaziland establishing their first shop at the Mall. Manzini is a growing town which services the industrial areas and the farmers in the region with agricultural supplies, plant, vehicles and service.

SWAZILAND INTERNATIONAL TRADE FAIR

A perfect forum for your products.

More than 160,000 visitors every year.

The fair usually starts at the end of August every year.

For further information contact us at:
PO BOX 877, MANZINI, SWAZILAND
TEL: 52324, 54242 FAX: 52324 TLX: 2232 WD

SWAZILAND TRADE FAIR

The Swaziland International Trade Fair exhibits annually in the last week of August and the first week of September attracting regional and international participants in the exhibition of their products. Participants from the Republic of China and the African States regularly show their products at this Fair. Swaziland maintains a tourist exhibition at which crafts and tourist information is available. Commerce and Industry of the Kingdom feature the national products: sugar, wood pulp, cotton, minerals and manufactured goods which maintain the economy of Swaziland.

Swaziland Int. Trade Fair, P.O.Box 877, Manzini, Tel: 52324/54242, Fax: 52324

THE HUB AND SPAR SUPERMARKET

The Hub, Manzini's newest shopping centre, is located close to Swaziland Warehouse and Jumbo Discount Store. Travel down Nkoseluhlaza Street and turn left onto Mhlakuvane Street, the Hub is at the end of this street on the right. A highly selective group of shops and restaurants are here including Nando's Chickenland, Sailor Sam fast food fish take away, a Sewing Machine centre, ladies and men's boutiques, jewellery shop and many more. The Spar Supermarket is the anchor shop filled with every possible item the visitor could want. From groceries, fresh vegetables, fruit and meat to special imported foods, confectionary and teas. Visitors staying in self catering resorts will find this shop a real boon for everyday requirements.

Spar Supermarket, P.O. Box 112, Mbabane, Tel: 53875/53846, Fax: 46023

The Hub, Manzini

THE MOCAMBIQUE HOTEL AND RESTAURANT

Within walking distance in Mahleka Street is an hotel catering for visitors and local residents. Accommodation is reasonably priced, this is a popular hotel with visiting businessmen and contract personnel. Set within the hotel is the very popular Mocambique Restaurant where a friendly bar and Portuguese atmosphere create relaxation for dining in casual enjoyment. King, queen and medium prawns are the speciality of the house, as are chicken and fish cooked as only the Portuguese can. A fine selection of South African and Portuguese wines are available, plus those special liqueurs to round off an excellent meal. Visitors, seeking a warm informal venue where everyone meets, should book a table at the Mocambique Restaurant.

The Bhunu Mall, Manzini

The Mocambique Hotel and Restaurant, P.O. Box 417, Manzini, Tel: 52489/52586

Travel out of Manzini on the road towards Siteki on your left you will come to the The New George Hotel, well signposted, stop here for a while and enjoy the shopping of Manzini, the surrounding area and the business environment of Manzini and Matsapha.

MOÇAMBIQUE HOTEL
AND RESTAURANT
New rooms available at reasonable prices
Box 417, Manzini, Swaziland. Phone: 52489, 52586
Mahleka Street (Opposite the bus rank)

THE NEW GEORGE HOTEL

55 bedrooms all with ensuite bathrooms, telephone, T.V. with 2nd channel, all air conditioned, good conference facilities, swimming pool, a la carte restaurant, coffee shop.

This very well placed hotel has recently been completely refurbished and updated to a very high standard. Every room is air conditioned which is a boon in the hot summer months. The Grill Room a la carte restaurant offers tempting dishes and a quiet ambience after a busy day. Breakfast is served in the popular Coffee Shop as are light meals at lunch time. The new City Pub has a happy Pub atmosphere, great to meet old and new friends here, typical pub meals are also served here. This is a very good conference hotel, well placed and appointed to cater for large and small groups. The New George Hotel is just 500 metres from the facilities of the Manzini Club; tennis, golf, squash and horseriding nearby, all can be arranged by the hotel.

New George Hotel, P.O. Box 51, Manzini, Tel: 52061/4, Telex 2071 WD, Fax: 52061

Middleveld Flowers. Photo by Fotostudio

Reception at the New George Hotel

The New George Hotel

Modern air conditioned rooms with T.V., conference facilities, grill room, coffee shop

Centrally situated in MANZINI
P.O. Box 51, Manzini, Swaziland
Tel/Fax: (268) 52061

*Tradition lives in Swaziland —
in legend and
in culture.*

SWAZILAND
KINGDOM OF CONTRASTS AND TRADITION

Further details from:
SARTOC,
P.O. Box 600, Parklands,
Johannesburg 2121.
Tel: 011 788 0742,
Fax: 011 788 1200

Chapter 5

The South and West of Swaziland

The Journey from Mahamba Nhlangano	110
The Nhlangano Sun Hotel	111
The Grand Valley	111
The Journey from Nerston/Sandlane to Bhunya/Usutu	112
The Forester's Arms Hotel	113
Mhlambanyatsi	114
Meikles Mount	114
The Journey from Mhlambanyatsi and Mbabane	115
The Journey from Bhunya to Malkerns Valley	115
Rosecraft	116
The Journey from Malkerns to Mankayane and Nhlangano	116

The Nhlangano Sun Hotel & Casino

THE JOURNEY FROM MAHAMBA

Mahamba border post (OPEN FROM 07H00 TO 22H00) is one of the main entry points to the Kingdom. Close to Piet Retief, it is a pivotal area for export and import of goods to and from the railhead at Piet Retief. Visitors using this entry post travel along an excellent tar road towards the town of Nhlangano which is the main agricultural centre of the Shiselweni District.

NHLANGANO

In 1947 King Sobhuza II of Swaziland met King George of Great Britain, in this southern town. King George was accompanied by his wife Elizabeth and their two daughters, the elder later to become Queen Elizabeth II. The town was then called Geodgegun, however the name Nhlangano means "meeting place" to commemorate this historic meeting of the Kings.

The bar at the Nhlangano Hotel

The Two Kings meet at Nhlangano

THE NHLANGANO SUN HOTEL AND CASINO

48 air conditioned rooms ensuite bathrooms, radio, TV, telephone, private terrace, Casino, conference facilities for 80 persons.

A large picture within the bar of this very attractive and friendly hotel, depicts the meeting of King Sobhuza II with King George VI. The Nhlangano Sun is a hotel offering very personal and cheerful service to the visitor. Set in 45 acres of spectacular grounds, the hotel looks over the Makhosini Valley. This is a wonderful place for walking, riding, fishing or just lazing and enjoying the magnificent view from the pool terrace. The chalet style rooms are joined by interleading walkways focusing on the central building to the Makhosini Restaurant and Two Kings bar. The staff are outstanding in their care and attention to detail; from a casual lunch or barbeque on the lawns surrounding the pool, to a formal dinner in the a la carte restaurant. There is a Casino, a cinema showing current films and a disco. Sporting facilities:golf, tennis, swimming and horse riding.

Nhlangano Sun Hotel, P. Bag Nhlangano, Tel: 78211,Telex 2089 WD, Fax: 78402.

THE GRAND VALLEY

The route towards Hlatikulu and Manzini is possibly the most picturesque in the Kingdom; travelling through the middleveld, up steep hills and down into valleys. Part of the route runs beside the Mkhondo River, through the forested area of Shiselwini and past the rolling agricultural area of this very pretty district. Little wonder that the first Swazi clans chose this area as their capital, the region between Dwaleni, Nhlangano and Hlatikulu rises from the lowveld to middleveld where the grazing was mixed and rainfall consistent. This is a truly magic area to stop for a picnic or barbeque, wide spreading trees line the river and if you climb up to Hlatikulu, the view down to the valley is breathtaking. It is 97 kms from Mahamba to the main Mbabane - Manzini road. As you approach this main road, the scenery becomes less dramatic and the population heavier. For visitors who have a short time in Swaziland a trip to Nhlangano is very worthwhile especially when it is combined with a picnic lunch or visit to the Nhlangano Sun and Casino Hotel who specialise in personal and friendly service to visitors.

The river and road run side by side in the Grand Valley

THE JOURNEY FROM NERSTON/SANDLANE TO MHLAMBANYATI RETURNING TO MBABANE

The Usutu Forest. Photo by Fotostudio

The forested highlands of Swaziland greet the visitor as you pass through this entry gate to the Kingdom; the Nerston/Sandlane post is the most direct for travellers coming from the Reef. The great Usutu forest is one of the largest man-made forests in the world, hectares of trees cover sweeping mountain sides. Hidden in the valley are streams, rivers, caves and ravines which have remained unspoilt and unchanged for centuries. Travel the 34 kms from the border to Bhunya where the Usutu Pulp company is situated. The Usutu forests cover 65,000 hectares of land within which are numerous forest paths, rivers and dams stocked with bass and trout. Fishermen may obtain licenses from the Foresters Arms Hotel which is our next stop within this chapter.

Forester's Arms Lounge. Photo by Fotostudio

Foresters Arms Restaurant. Photo by Fotostudio

Gloriously situated 25 km from Mbabane on tarred scenic road. Trout fishing, nature trails, horse riding, golf, pool, sauna - even tandem cycling!

Luxury accommodation, imaginative cooking and Victorian picnics. Homebaked breads, teas, lunches (specially Sundays!).

P.O. Box 14, Mhlambanyati, Swaziland.
Tel: (268) 26084, 73477, 74177, 45707 Fax: (268) 74051

THE FORESTER'S ARMS

24 rooms with private bath, television, M.Net, BBC, CNN and video channel, Sauna, swimming pool, Conference facilities and meeting rooms, fishing, nearby horseriding. Only 40 minutes from the Nerston/Sandlane border and only 25 kms from Mbabane, the visitor finds The Forester's Arms. This country hotel offers quality, peace and personal service in an intimate environment. Owned and managed by the vivacious Ruth Buck, there is great attention to detail and genuine concern for guests' comfort. From the chintz covered easy chairs in the lounge to the cosy bar and candle-lit dining room, this very pretty and secluded hotel never fails to ease the cares of busy city life. The Forester's Arms is only 20 minutes drive from Mbabane on the newly tarred road and 30 minutes from the Casino and nightlife of the Ezulwini Valley. Renowned for an excellent table and Sunday lunch, your host personally ensures that each menu is attractive and appetising. Visitors would do well to stay awhile and enjoy the peace, splendid setting and facilities offered by this country hotel. Swimming and a sauna are all here, plus a quality video selection. Trout and bass fishing in the many dams within the forests is both relaxing and rewarding. Enjoy the tonic of a mountain getaway, the romance of Forester's Arms is yet another wonderful surprise awaiting you The Golf Course adjoins the property and visitors are made most welcome, tennis and squash are nearby. Book for a few days at this delightful hotel, the wonderful welcome and stunning views are always there.

Forester's Arms Hotel, P.O. Box 14, Mhlambanyati, Tel: 26084, 74377, 74177, 45707 Fax: 74051

MEIKLES MOUNT

A world apart, unbelievably beautiful, where Nature dominates and you can enjoy the quiet comfort of a self-contained cottage, superbly equipped and serviced.

Walking, Climbing, Fishing, Horseriding, Other Activities

P.O. Box 13,
Mhlambanyatsi
Telephone 74110

MHLAMBANYATI

Mhlambanyati means "Watering Place of the Buffaloes" and was named after a famous Swazi Regiment who rested there.

Travel slowly through the village of Mhlambanyati which houses the employees of Usutu Pulp and contains shops, schools, churches, sports facilities and a clinic. Continue along the main tar road through the village and in 5 km you will see a sign pointing to the right which is a shorter and very scenic route towards Malkerns and Manzini. This is a gravel road but very rewarding to those who drive carefully wishing to enjoy the drop from the highveld through the forests to the middleveld of the Malkerns Valley. Enquire as to the state of the road during the rainy season.

6 kms further travelling on the main tar road and some 18 kms before Mbabane, you will note a sign post pointing on the right to Meikles Mount. Just 4 kms along this road brings you to the gate of Meikles Mount estate.

MEIKLES MOUNT

The Meikles Mount Estate

Set within its own 300 hectare estate which rises to 1341 metres at mountain top and drops to the river's edge at 884m, Meikles Mount offers a variety of landscapes, vegetation and experiences. Meikles Mount is a privately owned hideaway where a complete break from the humdrum of life is assured. There are endless footpaths, in superb country with the opportunity to fish for bream, bass, yellows and barbel and it is a birdwatcher's paradise. The visitor may climb to the top of Mhlane Mountain or the Mount and look across the Usutu Forests to Mlilwane

Nature Sanctuary. The Usushwana River invites you to sit at its edge, enjoy the waterfalls, fish in its depths and experience the tranquility of Meikles Mount. Within the estate are a number of fully equipped, thatched cottages with lounge/dining room, well appointed kitchen, bathroom and either 1,2 or 3 double bedrooms plus a carport and barbeque area. Meikles Mount was created many years ago and experience has proved that you need at least two nights to properly enjoy this wonderful part of Swaziland. Bookings are for a minimum of 2 nights and many stay longer. This is a treasure trove of experiences for the entire family. A large swimming pool, playhouse, croquet lawn, badminton, tennisette, swingball and a sandpit for the very young are all set here behind the cottages. A cook maid is available to look after you, who can shop on your behalf from the estate shop, cook and baby sit. A resident stable of horses is on the estate, lessons are available for the uninitiated, outrides, trails and hacks can be organised which is a wonderful way to view the surrounding forests, streams and mountains. This is truly a haven of natural beauty and peace.

Meikles Mount, P.O. Box 13, Mhlambanyati, Tel: 74110

Your journey now returns to the main tar road and towards the capital, Mbabane. This road has been completely re-surfaced since the last issue of this guide, a well structured tar road giving very easy access to this very beautiful part of Swaziland. You will cross the Little Usutu which feeds into Luphohlo Dam on your right. This Dam is used for windsurfing, and sailing by local residents; no power boats are allowed. Only 5 kms from the Capital it is a popular area at weekends and over public holidays. This fully circular route includes some of the most spectacular scenery in Swaziland. The entire journey is 98 kms and takes a comfortable 2 hours, stop for a picnic beside the dam and travel gently towards Mbabane to browse and shop.

THE JOURNEY FROM BHUNYA TO MALKERNS VALLEY

The visitor arriving through the Nerston/Sandlane border drives to Bhunya and then turns left towards Mhlambanyati and Mbabane or right towards Malkerns, Manzini or Mbabane. The area between Bhunya and Malkerns is undulating and primarily

Stark, beautiful mountains. Photo by Steve Hall

Rosecraft

PURE MOHAIR PRODUCTS
FROM SWAZILAND
HANDSPUN, HANDWOVEN

curtaining,
fabrics,
clothing,
carpets

PO Box 192, Malkerns
Kingdom of Swaziland
Tel: (+268) 53915 Fax: (+268) 85033

agricultural. On the right you travel beside the Great Usutu River on its route towards Lubombo in the east and eventually to the sea in Mocambique. Pineapple fields across the Usutu flourish in the middleveld climate. Rolling grasslands and contented cattle are plentiful in this valley; beware of crossing cattle and goats as you drive towards Malkerns.

21 kms from Bhunya on the right is a turning to Mankayane. Continue for a further 7 kms and pass the University of Swaziland on your right which houses the Faculty of Agriculture. Either turn left into the Malkerns village or continue straight on passing Swazi Candles on the right and Baobab Batik on the left. The road joins the main Mbabane/Malkerns road in 5kms.

THE JOURNEY FROM MALKERNS TO MANKAYANE AND NHLANGANO

Retrace your journey to the Mankayane turnoff, which is on your left. Turn here and cross the bridge over the Great Usutu; 1 km on the left you will note a gravel road leading to Rosecraft Mohair Products.

ROSECRAFT

18 kms from the turnoff after travelling over rolling hills and what seems like the top of the world, you will find Rosecraft signposted on your right. Rosecraft has developed a completely self sufficient mohair industry from the farm and workshops at Mankayane. They rear their own Angora goats and Merino sheep, shear regularly, sort, comb, dye, spin and weave the most exquisite mohair fabrics and wool garments and rugs. Any colour combination is possible and Rosecraft products are exported worldwide. Visitors are asked to telephone prior to visiting Rosecraft.
Rosecraft, P.O.Box 192, Malkerns, Tel: 53915, Fax: 85033

The route to Mankayane is truly magnificent as you climb high into the mountains and through the pine trees of the Usutu forests. Deep ravines, rolling valleys and stark peaks rise and fall on both sides of the road. The route to Mankayane from the Bhunya/Malkerns road is 27 kms. As you enter Mankayane you drop fairly steeply into this small town. A police station, garages and supermarket are here plus a small hotel. The road continues through Manzini, Sicunusa where there is a border post (Hours 08h00 to 18h00), Gege another border post (hours 08h00 to 16h00) and eventually arrives after 80 kms in Nhlangano where you may stop at the Nhlangano Sun and then return to Manzini through the Grand Valley. This circular route from the Malkerns turnoff and return is 194 kms and will take approximately 4 hours. From the turnoff to Mankayane to Nhlangano, the road is gravel and can be slippery in summer.

Chapter 6

The South East of Swaziland

The Journey from Lavumisa to Manzini	118-127
The Riverside Motel	119
The New Bend Inn	120
Ubombo Ranches	120
Mkhaya Nature Reserve	121
Contribution by Ted Reilly	125-126
St Joseph's Mission	127
The Journey from Lavumisa to Nhlangano	127

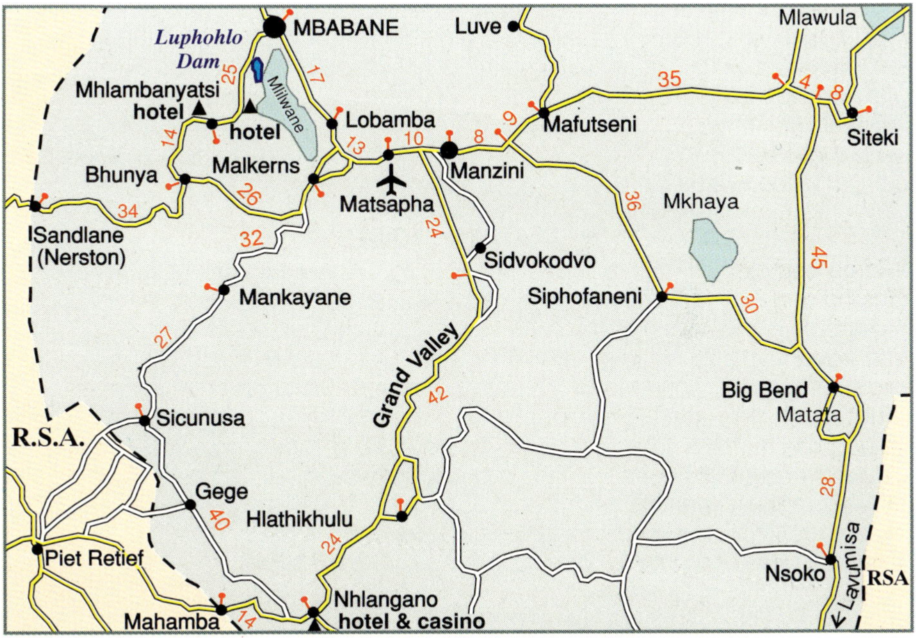

ESTABLISHED 1896   BIG BEND   TEL: 36144

* BUTCHERY
* FRUIT & VEGETABLES
* BAKERY
* GROCERIES
* PERISHABLES
* MEN'S CLOTHING
* LADIES' CLOTHING
* CHILDREN'S CLOTHING
* BABYWEAR
* MATERIALS
* SHOES
* PHOTOGRAPHIC
* RADIOS
* ARMS & AMMUNITION
* HARDWARE
* BUILDING MATERIALS
* TIMBER
* WHOLESALE CASH'N'CARRY
* FURNITURE STORE
* GARAGE SPARES
* GARAGE WORKSHOP
* PETROL STATION
* BULK FEEDS
* DRY CLEANERS
* BOTTLE STORE
* RECORD STORE
* TAKE AWAYS

THE JOURNEY FROM LAVUMISA TO MANZINI

Motorists arriving from Natal cross into Swaziland at Golela/Lavumisa border post (open 07h00 - 22h00). This is a major route into the Kingdom; the road through to the main centres of Big Bend, Manzini and Mbabane is fully tarred and passes through the lowveld of Swaziland, following the border with Natal and travels through cotton and farming country. Within the tiny town of Lavumisa is a modest country hotel offering overnight accommodation and simple meals. From Big Bend northwards the border is shared with Mozambique. Big Bend is only 54 kms from the border and is situated next to the Great Usutu River.

MATATA STORES

A large complex of shops is located at Matata which is just 47 kms from the border crossing and 3 kms before you arrive at the Riverside Motel. Visitors who are camping or self catering will find Matata Stores very interesting. Turn off left onto a gravel road and travel 4 kms to this large marketing area which caters for most local needs. A large garage and workshop which undertakes most repair and maintenance work is situated on the right of the complex, this may be a welcome haven to the beleagured motorist. There is a post office, a bank, a video and electrical shop, dry cleaners and bottle store. The enormous supermarket sells almost everything; groceries, butchery, bakery, photographic processing, clothing, curtaining, cooking utensils, materials and building supplies are all available here.
Matata Stores, P.O.Box 1, Matata, Tel: 36144, Fax: 36587

RIVERSIDE HOTEL & RESTAURANT
with NIGHTCLUB

on the main road north just before Big Bend,
next to Shell Petrol Station
- the ideal stopover, Portuguese style cooking
18 ensuite bedrooms, all with carports.
Bottle store open 6 days, 9.00 am - 7.00 pm
P.O. Box 110, Big Bend, Tel: (268) 36012, Fax: (268) 36032

RIVERSIDE MOTEL AND RESTAURANT

10 ensuite bedrooms, secure carports, swimming pool, restaurant, patio, nightclub. On the right, just beyond the Shell Garage and only 50 kms from the border is situated the Riverside Motel and Restaurant. This motel is finished to a very high standard and is a most welcome venue after a long hot drive. Each room is very private and has its own carport, there is a roof garden, swimming pool and a welcoming bar above the pool and garden. The restaurant overlooks the Usutu River and Portuguese cuisine is the hallmark of this motel. Residents from the surrounding area make the Riverside restaurant their regular eating and meeting place. Travellers may wish to have their vehicles checked over before continuing their exploration of Swaziland; a garage and workshop is right next door. Below is a nightclub which will please night owls, however this is far enough away from the bedrooms not to interfere with sleep. Stay awhile in this very pleasant motel and enjoy the stillness of the lowveld where the pace of life is easy and the proximity to Mkhaya is very convenient.

Riverside Motel and Restaurant, P.O. Box 110, Big Bend, Tel: 36012, Fax: 36032

The Riverside Motel, Restaurant and Garage

LUBOMBO LOBSTER RESTAURANT
AT THE FOOT OF THE LUBOMBO MOUNTAIN RANGE

Friendly bar, seafood, fish cooked in that special Portuguese style Try the fantastic Highway Hen cooked over open coals. Complemented with good imported Portuguese wine.

Tel/Fax:
(+268) 36308

Just off the main Road

Open 7.00 am - till late

Your journey continues towards Big Bend which is situated left off the main road towards the bend in the River.

UBOMBO RANCHES LTD

Set within its own 6000 hectare estate, Ubombo Ranches grows, mills and refines sugar for the Nation and for export. Acres of waving cane stretch towards the horizon flourishing in the heat of the Lowveld. Ubombo has the only sugar refinery within the Kingdom and all of the domestic sugar required for Swaziland is produced at Ubombo. Ubombo Ranches also raise a herd of beef cattle suitable for domestic and export needs. The staff and employees of the company are well catered for as a 45 bed Cottage Hospital is maintained by the company providing medical care for staff and for local residents. Excellent sporting facilities exist at the Ubombo Recreation Club which is on the road leading into Big Bend. Pass the Ubombo Recreation Club on the left and stop at the Bend Inn on your right.

THE NEW BEND INN HOTEL

16 bedrooms, 8 with baths ensuite, 8 with showers ensuite, telephone and radio in rooms, TV lounge, driver's rooms, restaurant, swimming pool, outside entertainment area.
This family hotel serves the local sugar industry and acts as a meeting point for visitors to the lowveld. Located at the bend of the Usutu, the dining room and verandah face the river. An open air bar is set close to the swimming pool offering bar snacks and the dining is good at this country hotel. Rolling, picturesque gardens border the river and complete the

THE NEW BEND INN HOTEL

* Swimming Pool
* A-la-Carte Restaurant
* Evening Take-Aways
* Air Conditioned Rooms Overlooking Great Usutu River
* Indoor and Outdoor Bars
* Snooker Tables

Tel: (268) 36111 Fax: (268) 36112
Telegrams "BEND INN"
P.O. Box 37, Big Bend, Swaziland

tranquil atmosphere. In 1984 when Cyclone Domoina hit this area, the low level bridge was completely covered by floods and debris, unfortunately the high level bridge took the full brunt of tree trunks, branches and river mud, it buckled and the road is now carried across the Usutu further south of Big Bend.

The New Bend Inn Hotel, P.O. Box 37, Big Bend, Tel: 36111/2 Fax: 36364,

Leave Big Bend and travel towards Manzini. You will pass the Big Bend Sugar Mill and Tambuti Citrus Estates. On the right is a newly tarred road leading to Siteki which from this point is 56 kms away. Continue for approximately 30 kms from Big Bend and you cross the river and the railway line at Phuzumoya Station. Here is the meeting point and pick up area for those visiting Mkhaya Game Reserve.

MKHAKA GAME RESERVE

Mkhaya Game Reserve is a very special place in the Kingdom of Swaziland. It is a private Game Reserve owned and designated as a refuge for endangered species by Swaziland's eminent conservationist Ted Reilly. Covering an area of 6250 hectares, Mkhaya provides the visitor with rare opportunities to see black and white rhino at very close quarters. Other species weaned back to Swaziland are Tsessebe, Roan Antelope and Elephant which are all thriving and secure within this well structured sanctuary. The Sable Antelope breeding programme is flourishing, young Sable are settling well in Mkhaya which is a great reward as Sable are among the very endangered species rarely seen in game reserves elsewhere. Visitors are normally able to view these tall, magnificent, rare animals silhouetted against the thicker tree canopies.

Entry to Mkhaya is by prior arrangement only. Game rangers will meet and collect you in open landrovers while you leave your own vehicle in safe keeping at the Reserve or arrive as part of an organized tour. Mkhaya vehicles are well adapted to

Rhino and Elephant at Mkhaya. Photo courtesy of Big Game Parks

Superb Sable Antelope bull, part of the Mkhaya endangered species programme. Photo courtesy of Big Game Parks

Guided walking safaris at Mkhaya Game Reserve. Photo courtesy of Big Game Parks.

circumvent the roads, rivers and shrub bush within the sanctuary. From the moment you enter Mkhaya you may well see wild animals and especially the imperilled rhino at very close range. The enthusiasm and dedication of both Ted and Liz Reilly in their determination to conserve and replenish the endangered species is gradually bearing fruit. Mkhaya is a new Reserve, destined to nurture and increase the numbers of the Rhino, Elephant, Nyala, Buffalo, Eland and Roan Antelope within the Kingdom. In 1987 Ted arranged the difficult passage of the very rare black rhino from the Zambezi river to Swaziland. In exchange for white rhino, 6 black rhino were spirited from the poaching areas of the Zambezi into Mkhaya. Since their arrival, the black rhino have settled in, developed and become accustomed to the presence of interested observers.

Mkhaya is acclaimed by the Worldwide Fund for Nature as a secure and properly managed sanctuary for endangered species. At the cost of high fences, tall watch towers and ever vigilant rangers, Mkhaya has a large herd of Nguni cattle descended from the original breed which accompanied the first people to enter Swaziland. Nguni cattle are hardy, well suited to the rigours of the African climate and largely immune to disease. They survive the heat, drought and withstand the tsetse fly and foot and mouth disease. Introduced into Mlilwane and brought to Mkhaya, the Nguni cattle now graze alongside zebra, buffalo and wildebeest. Snatched from very possible oblivion as the Nguni were interbred with European breeds, His Majesty King Sobhuza II expressed very genuine concern at the dwindling numbers of this hardy breed. Now, the Nguni flourish, restored to the Kingdom and form an essential economic ingredient of Mkhaya Game Reserve.

Mkhaya offers a fully inclusive African experience. Luxury tented accommodation set in the dense bush within the reserve contributes to the feeling of being at one with Nature. This is a haven for the lover of wildlife; a complete bush experience in comfortable beds and cosy tents. The camp is set close to the river bed, riverine birds, hardwood trees and soft river grass sounds are close at hand from early morning.

Each tent sleeps two within a very well furnished interior. Indigenous woods make up the bed bases, kists, side tables and chairs. Most of the luxury tents have en suite facilities of hot water showers and flushing toilets, others have these facilities located nearby. Lighting is by paraffin lamps and staff are on hand to point the way towards the central camp areas. Here, cooking over an open camp fire produces the unusual and authentic in African dishes. Homemade bread, venison, homemade boerwoers, honey, fresh vegetables and fruit all play their part in the Mkhaya experience.

Game drives in open landrovers are organized in the early morning before breakfast. Explore the thick bush for the elusive tsessebe, catch a glimpse of the statuesque giraffe, spot the shy zebra and wildebeest hiding behind the hardwood trees. Overhead see the high flying, soaring bateleur travelling kilometres every day and the white backed vulture perching high in his tree protecting his young and looking for carrion.

Return for a very substantial breakfast cooked on the camp fire. After breakfast take a game walk with an experienced Mkhaya guide, you may chance upon a rhino or elephant at close quarters and truly appreciate the grandeur, majesty and immensity of these endangered animals. Mkhaya offer day trips which include lunch and landrover rides and group tours can also be arranged.

Mkhaya Game Reserve, P.O. Box 234, Mbabane, Tel: 44541, Fax: 40957 a/h & weekends Tel: 34371/61591/2/3, Fax: 61594

Traditional Swazi catering at Mkhaya's bushcamp. Photo courtesy of Big Game Parks

THE RETURN OF RESIDENT ELEPHANT (January 1986 and April 1987)

Young bull elephant at Mkhaya. Photo by Big Game Parks

Resident elephants disappeared from Swaziland in response to heavy hunting pressure at the turn of the century. The last record was of two bulls in 1954, which entered the Kingdom from the north and then heading south they crossed the Usuthu River and on downstream into Mocambique. It was therefore an historic milestone when in January 1986 and again in April 1987, Swaziland was blessed with the successful introduction of elephants to Mkhaya and Hlane.

Two young elephants were introduced from the Transvaal in January 1986 to become the first resident elephants in the Kingdom for the better part of a century. At Mkhaya, these two elephants were closely watched for a year to determine whether the reintroduction of the species to Swaziland was feasible.

An application was made to National Parks Board of South Africa, who responded most positively and allocated eight as a donation provided the cost of capture was paid for, and the other ten were offered at a special price of E800 each. Dr. Anton Rupert, picked up the cost of the entire operation, and presented His Majesty King Mswati III with a birthday gift of ten of the elephants to be released on Hlane - a magnanimous gesture which was graciously accepted. Dr. Rupert also met the cost of the other eight, which actually caused mortality. We lost two animals and would have undoubtedly lost more had we not separated the elephants into sizes. Once we did this, the problem ceased.

Reproduced by kind permission of Ted Reilly.

MKHAYA RIVER RAFTING

White-water rafting is the newest and most exciting outdoor activity in the Kingdom. Since its launch in December 1991, it has been incredibly popular with both visitors to the Kingdom and local residents alike.

The launch was the culmination of months of exploration and planning, during which time the many rivers of Swaziland were scoured for a suitable stretch of hi-volume white-water. An ideal stretch was found on the Great Usutu river, where, with its volume already swelled by the Mkondo, Ngwempisi and Lusushwana rivers, it is forced to forge its way between the Mabukabuka and Bulunga mountains. The river winds its way through a moonscape of smooth rocks, swirling around unseen obstacles and plunging down spectacular rapids. Finally, in a fury of thundering spray, the Great Usutu throws itself over its final barrier and plunges 10m into a boiling pot below.

It is in this unique wilderness area that the trips are run. A typical outing starts when visitors meet their guides at the Phuzumoya turnoff to Mkhaya Game Reserve. Transferred into open landrovers, they are transported upstream, with the road weaving its way between boulders and through 'dongas'. Visitors are also able to meet the friendly people of Siphofaneni, who wave as the procession passes their homes.

On reaching the put-in point, equipment is unloaded and rafters are fitted with lifejackets and helmets. Then onto the riverbank, where the trip-leader instructs everyone on rafting technique, safety and the river itself. Questions are asked, answered, and as soon as everyone is confident at facing what lies ahead, the adventure begins.

Quietly the Usutu slips into the lunar-landscape of the Bulungapoort, and rafters crane their necks to catch the first glimpse of approaching rapids. The guides ready their crews and suddenly all hell breaks loose: "HIGHSIDE! BACK-TO-POSITION! HUG-THE-ROCK! HOLD ON! EDDY-OUT, EDDY OUT!!! The instructions come hard and fast, the raft punches through waves of tumbling water, bounces off menacing rocks and glides into the pool below. Wild, wet and bewitched the rafters emerge, adrenalin pumping and ready to face the next challenge.

On reaching the waterfall, the raft is picked up and portaged around. A short break is taken and a well-earned lunch enjoyed. Then, with the waterfall left in the background, the afternoon starts with a different type of offering. Here the river flattens out, and the peace is only disturbed by frequent sightings of the Usutu's renowned "flat-dog", the ever present crocodile. Whether sunning themselves on a sandbank, or lying semi-submerged in the water, they are a sight to be seen. So on this restful note, with the sun setting over the river, the trip winds to its end.

Absolutely NO experience is necessary and interested people need not be physical fitness fanatics. At no time is anyone ever expected to do something they are uneasy about. There is always the option to walk around the bigger rapids, and people often do. Ideal for families, groups of friends and corporate bodies; rafting is a sure way to cement friendships and strengthen teamwork. Mkhaya's unique bush camp is the perfect place to overnight, and from where to plan your daily adventures. Trips can be booked daily throughout the year, with large 8 man rafts used in the summer months and smaller 2 man "croc" rafts in the drier months. Abseiling with mountaineering equipment down a 18m cloff at the Bulunga Falls is an optional extra

adrenalin boost. Whether being expertly rowed by a friendly oarsman, or paddling as a team, co-ordinated by a guide, the bottom line is FUN!
Reproduced by kind permission of Ted Reilly

Leave Mkhaya Nature Reserve and drive towards Manzini passing through Siphofaneni until you reach the junction at Hhelehhele which is 38 kms from the Mkhaya turnoff. Turn left towards Manzini which is only 8 kms from this junction.

ST JOSEPH'S MISSION

About 5 kms beyond the Helehele turnoff which points right towards Bid Bend and Lavumisa, continue on the main road towards Siteki and Lomahasha. On your left you will note an archway which is the entrance to St. Joseph's Mission. Here, handicapped men and women are taught vocational skills including weaving, sewing, carpentry, basketwork, fence making and tapestry. The Mission is run by an Italian Order of Fathers with assistance from Germany. Try to make time to visit the showrooms of this community of people. To watch the severely handicapped overcome the problems of handtools is remarkable. Fence making is undertaken by the blind who use fixed templates around which they wind and mould the wire to form intricate designs. The carpentry work is of a very high standard and St. Joseph's are requested by numerous schools to manufacture desks, chairs and benches. In addition beds, bunks and bookcases may be seen, ordered and purchased from the showroom. Smaller items include woven materials, small tapestries, basketware, table mats, clothes hangers and small toys. The prices are reasonable and the quality is high. St Joseph's now have a marketing outlet at Mantenga Crafts called the "Pine Corner". Here visitors will see a small range of their wooden furniture and weavings.

The Black Rhino. Photo by Big Game Parks

THE ROUTE FROM LAVUMISA TO NHLANGANO

There is a gravel road from Lavumisa to Nhlangano which covers 93 kms passing through Hluti, Mhlosheni and Dwaleni. It would be wise to enquire as to the condition of the road before leaving Lavumisa. However, this is a further opportunity to see the south east of Swaziland and connect with the route through the Grand Valley from Nhlangano to Manzini. For visitors who have the time, a circular journey from Manzini to Nhlangano, on to Lavumisa returning to Manzini via Big Bend and Hhelehhele encompasses the stillness of the lowveld and rising hills of the middleveld. The complete journey is 323 kms and a full day will allow a proper appreciation of this area.

THE SWAZILAND SUGAR INDUSTRY

The Swaziland Sugar Industry, established in 1956 when the total annual production was 57,000 tonnes, has dramatically expanded bringing production to about 457,268 tonnes in 1993/4. Cane cultivation and sugar manufacture is Swaziland's biggest industry directly employing 12,000 Swazis. Local sugar consumption represents 22% of production whereas the export market is valued at over E500 million. The Swaziland Sugar Association, representing equally the Cane Grower's Association and the Miller's Association spearheads the sales and marketing of all sugar. The Swaziland Sugar Industry is widely regarded as highly efficient and reliable in quality and service. The service to the Community includes an ambitious programme to alleviate water shortages in the Lowveld.

SUGAR SERVES SWAZILAND and is THE REAL SWAZI GOLD.

Swaziland Sugar Association, P.O. Box 445, Mbabane, Swaziland, Tel: 42646. Fax: 45005

Chapter 7

The North East of Swaziland

The Journey from Bordergate/ Mananga to Manzini	
The Sugar Estates	130
Tambankulu Club	131
Mbuluizi Nature Reserve	132
Mlawula Nature Reserve	134
Simunye Country Club & Nature Reserve	135
Hlane National Park	136
The Siteki Hotel	139
Circular drive of North East Swaziland	140

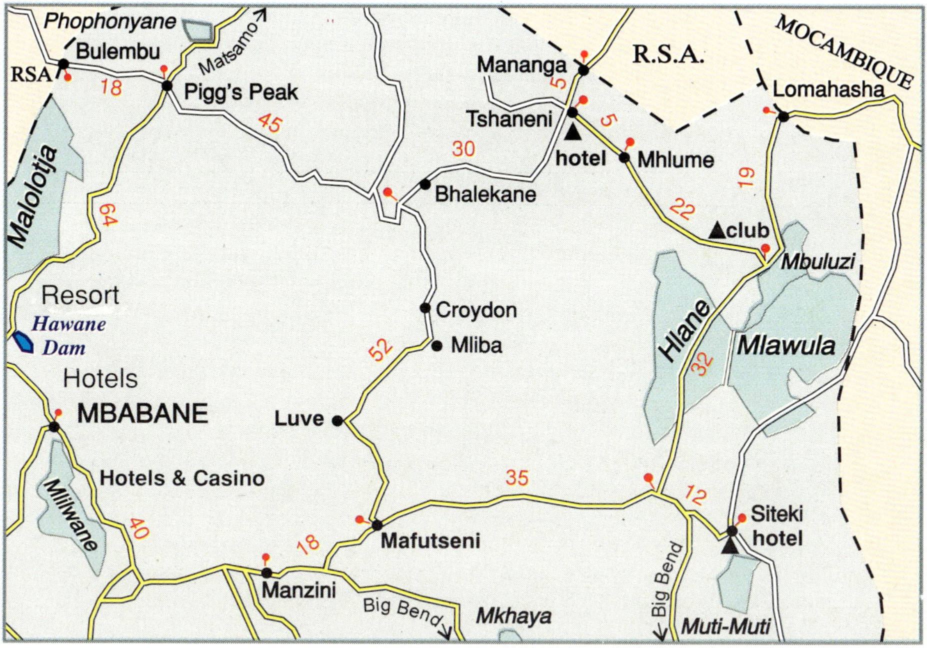

Entry into Swaziland from the Bordergate/Mananga border post (OPEN 08h00 - 18h00) is the closest to Lomahasha, Mozambique and a good entry point for those who have visited the Kruger National Park. The border post is very close to the Sand River Dam which is used by members and visitors for sailing and windsurfing.

THE IMPALA ARMS HOTEL

18 bedrooms, all ensuite, radio, some with TV. Residents bar, restaurant, cocktail bar. The Impala Arms is located in the town of Tshaneni situated in an imposing position at the top of the approach road.

The Impala Arms Hotel, P.O. Box 34, Tshaneni, Tel: 31244

THE SUGAR ESTATES

Visitors pass through hectares of waving sugar cane which provides employment, medical and educational care for thousands of Swazi people. Passing through Tshaneni, Mhlume, Tambankulu and Simunye, the visitor must note the order and neatness of these towns. Each town has its own shopping centre, church, schools, sporting clubs and medical facilities.

Sugar is the lifeline of this part of Swaziland. It is planted from a piece of cane, the eyes sprout and grow. They are fertilized, watered, and after 12 months of growth the cane is cut down. The cane is sent to the sugar mill for processing at Mhlume or Simunye within 24 hours the resulting sugar is then packed, marketed and despatched to every corner of the world. As Swaziland is part of the Preferential Trade Area, her exports to Europe are at preferential prices. Occasionally the sugar cane grows a grey tassle flower, which although attractive, is detrimental to the sugar growth. The top of the cane becomes hollow as the flower uses up some of the sucrose in the cane.

Sugar production has increased rapidly from 5,641 tons in 1958/59 to about 458,000 tons in 1994. Swaziland sugar is marketed worldwide, mostly exported to the E.C., some to U.S.A., Canada and the Orient, plus of course to the immediate region of East and Southern Africa; exports represent some E500 million, whereas local sugar consumption amounts to just 18% of production. Sugar growth and production are part of a natural cycle; The cane is planted, sugar harvested and processed, it is marketed, exported and the residue cane is ground into cattle feed which in turn fertilizes the soil for more growth. Raw sugar is also supplied to Swaziland industries encouraging them to add value by locally producing sweets, soft drinks and confectionery.

INYONI YAMI SWAZILAND IRRIGATION SCHEME

A sophisticated irrigation scheme exists in the North East of Swaziland which feeds water to the entire area from the Komati river 60 kms away. I.Y.S.I.S. operate a large estate at Tshaneni which is the first town the visitor enters having passed through the border at Mananga. Primarily a farming estate which covers 4,000 hectares of sugar cane and 500 hectares of citrus and deciduous fruits, I.Y.S.I.S. also run 500 head of beef cattle which is the largest ranch south east of the Limpopo river. Grapefruit, oranges and naatjies are cultivated for the European market and mangoes, peaches and lychees are also grown for export.

Mhlume Sugar Mill in North East Swaziland. Photo courtesy of Swaziland Sugar Association

The Sand River dam is upon the Estate which acts as a reservoir for the channelled water, used to irrigate in times of drought. Members of the Tshaneni Club have a Yacht Club there. The Tshaneni Club with its 9 hole Golf course, tennis, squash, swimming pool and library is a welcome venue for local residents. The estate also covers 20,000 hectares of lowveld bush which houses impala, zebra, waterbuck, nyala and a wonderful selection of bird life attracted to this area by the rising land of the Mananga Mountains.

MHLUME SUGAR COMPANY

Co-owned by the Commonwealth Development Corporation and Tibiyo Taka Ngwane on behalf of the nation, Mhlume is one of the oldest companies in Swaziland. Sugar cane is crushed at the mill on behalf of 316 small sugar farmers who belong to the Mhlume Mill group. This concern acts as a central point for local farmers who benefit from the Mill, expertise and experience of Mhlume personnel to process some of the best sugar cane in the world.

Travel along the main tarred road until you pass through the small town of Mhlume until you reach the estates of Tambankulu, 35 kms from the border.

TAMBANKULU UMBULUZI ESTATES

Tambankulu and Umbuluzi Estates are located across the Black Mbuluzi River and were originally devoted to cattle ranching. A fine herd of Brahmans was established, well suited to the semi-tropical climate of the Lowveld. Once the irrigation scheme was in place, sugar became the prime agricultural commodity. In 1978, 5,700 hectares of Umbuluzi Estates was sold to the Royal Swaziland Sugar Corporation and the balance cultivated as sugar to be milled at nearby Simunye Mill. Visitors are welcome to tour the estates which also grow top quality citrus fruit for the European, Japanese and Middle Eastern markets.

Ensuite accommodation at moderate rates

Tennis, Swimming, Gym, Snooker,
á la Carte Restaurant, well stocked bar.
All guests receive Top Flight treatment.
Dorrie Litschka personally supervises.

Visitors are welcome to tour the
Five Star Estate and Citrus Packhouse.
Three Nature Reserves
within fifteen minutes drive.
Situated 35kms from Bordergate Border.
Casual visitors are equally welcome

Tambankulu Recreational Club
Phone: (268) 38111 Fax: (268) 38213

The Tambankulu Club welcomes visitors as temporary members and offers excellent overnight accommodation, a full a la carte restaurant offering quality dishes and complemented by resonably priced wine and excellent sporting facilities. These include snooker, golf, squash, bowls and a fully equipped gym. A very welcome stop for visitors who enjoy a Club atmosphere and wish to rest between Natal and Kruger National Park or Mozambique. The access road to the Club is fully tarred and Tambankulu have a registered airstrip.

Tambankulu Estates, Private Bag Mhlume, Tel: 38111, Fax: 38213

MBULUZI NATURE RESERVE

Continue for a further 3 kms on the main Lomahasha-Manzini Road, you have now travelled 39 kms. Turn right towards Manzini and on your left is the entrance gate to Mbuluzi Nature Reserve which is managed by Tamabankulu Estates.

This very beautiful, unexplored area with virgin grasslands and thick tambouti and leadwood forests is a feast for sore eyes. The tall and thick riverine stretches of land alongside the Mlawula river have been designated as private land for interested investors. Each area of land has broad or distant view of the river and the entire reserve is destined to be preserved and improved with regards to game, bird, tree and plant species. The Mbuluzi Reserve adjoins the Mlawulu and Simunye Reseves all of which are havens for the beleagered wild life of Africa. There are small herds of giraffe, wildebeest, ostrich, zebra, kudu, baboon and of course impala in Mbuluzi Nature Reserve and an abundance of varied birdlife and the aim is to increase and improve these herds whilst upgrading their habitat.

Details from Tambankulu Club, Tel: 38111

Herd of young giraffe at Mbuluzi Nature Reserve

MLAWULA NATURE RESERVE

This extensive reserve is set below and upon the Lubombo Mountains which form a natural boundary between Swaziland and Mozambique. The Lubombo Mountains are volcanic in structure and altitudes range from 573m at the highest point to 76m at the eastern end of the Mbuluzi River. It is in the Lubombo area that the earliest known record of man was established. Early Stone Age tools dating back over one million years have been found along the river beds.

Within this diverse area live the unique Lubombo Ironwoods which shade the rare species of cycad forest found nowhere else in the world, plus other species of flora and game. Visitors may well see impala, nyala, kudu, waterbuck, zebra, wildebeest and white rhino. The shy oribi, red duiker and samango monkey may need greater perseverance, they are more likely to be spotted on foot or from a Landrover tour. Guided walks and Landrover tours are available and visitors may use canoes or dinghies on the Mbuluzi, but must obtain permission from the warden first. An interesting feature of Mlawula is the "Vulture Restaurant"; game and stock carcasses are brought to this specific place and visitors may watch the ensuing cleaning up operation by resident vultures. This takes place close to the Emangceni Hide when visitors may have to wait for quite a long period before the vultures appear. Visitors are requested to check with the Senior Warden prior to arriving at Mlawula as to the availability of stock and the fee which is charged for this facility and transport.

There are a number of self-guided hiking trails; the Mathewu Trail which runs near the Mbuluzi River is only 3 kms in length. Visitors may take a guide book to spot the botany, geology and animal life in the area, but please be very careful of crocodiles when walking close to the riverbeds.

There are two camping grounds at Mlawula: the Siphiso Campground which is located on the banks of the Siphiso River and is suitable for tents and caravans; there is an ablution block, baths, showers, toilets and a washing up area. Visitors must bring their own provisions, tents, bedding and towels. Each site has braai facilities and firewood is available.

The Mbuluzi Campground next to the Mbuluzi river has an open reed-enclosed shower with hot water, a thatched shelter and a pit toilet. A new, fully equipped tented camp has been established with three tents accommodating two beds each, bedding, towels, crockery, cutlery and cooking facilities are provided, however, there is no fridge at present.

Young kudu hide in the bush of North East Swaziland

MLAWULA NATURE RESERVE
SWAZILAND NATIONAL TRUST COMMISSION

Beautiful Nature Reserve situated in rugged countryside

Fully furnished tented camp
Game viewing,
Large camping sites,
Hiking trails,
and birdwatching.

Opening times:
Winter: 7.00 am - 6.00 pm
Summer: 6.30 am - 6.30 pm

For more information contact:
P.O. Box 312, Simunye, Swaziland
Tel: (268) 38885 Bookings: P.O. Box 100, Lobamba. Tel: (268) 61178/9 Fax: 61875

This is a wonderland for birdwatchers where over 300 species have been spotted. A bird checklist plus vertebrate and tree checklists are available from the Reserve. **Mlawula Nature Reserve, P.O. Box 312, Simunye, Tel: 38885 or P.O. Box 100, Lobamba. Tel: 61178/9 ,61516, 61151. Fax: 61875.**

Return to the main Lomahasha-Manzini Road and travel for a further 10 kms, toward Manzini and the town of Simunye. Turn left at Simunye (Lusoti Village) towards the Plaza, turn right into 5th Avenue and the Simunye Club entrance is on your left at the intersection with Hornbill Road.

SIMUNYE COUNTRY CLUB

The Simunye Country Club is a very welcome stopping point for travellers visiting the north east of Swaziland, the Kruger National Park and of course the Sugar Estates of this area. The Club has single and double ensuite accommodation, full airconditioning, a wonderful a la carte restaurant and extensive sporting facilities. Simunye offfers visitors the opportunity to enjoy Club temporary membership, to mix with the local residents and to learn some more about this very important region. Adjoining the Simunye Sugar Company land is the Simunye Nature Reserve which occupies part of an area between Mbuluzi and Mlawula Nature Reserves. Game wanders between these three reserves at present. Simunye Nature Reserve has embarked on a rehabilitation programme to maintain roads, control erosion and bush encroachment, improvement of recreational facilities and the correct management of fauna and its habitat. Four picnic spots have been created and a walking trail is in place running alongside the length of the Mlawula river. Animal species include warthog, wilde-

SIMUNYE
COUNTRY CLUB

PO Box 30 or 1, Simunye,
Kingdom of Swaziland
Tel/Fax: (+268) 52646 ext 2147
Tel: (+268) 38600 ext 2012

* Single & Double Accommodation, all Ensuite with Airconditioning.
* Conferences Catered for.
* Full a la Carte Menus for Lunch and Dinner
* Extensive Wine List.
* Tuesday, Thursday & Sundays Lunch time Special Table d'Hote Menu
* Golf, Tennis, Snooker, Swimming.
* Company Sports Weekends
* 20 Minutes to the Mocambique Border.

beest, zebra, baboon, leopard, jackal plus nyala, impala, kudu, duiker and hyena. Simunye Nature Reserve has over 250 different species of birdlife and varying habitats to suit the vegatation, fauna and flora.

**Simunye Country Club and Nature Reserve, P.O. Box 1, Simunye,
Tel: 52646,38600, Fax: 52646**

Leave Simunye and travel towards Manzini; on the far right you will see the Simunye Sugar Mill. On the right you will find a sign post pointing to Hlane Royal National Park, turn right here and travel a further kilometre to the main gate and entrance to the Ndlovu Camp.

HLANE ROYAL NATIONAL PARK

Hlane Royal National Park is the largest game reserve in the Kingdom covering a conservation area of 30,000 hectares. Hlane is held in trust for the nation by His Majesty King Mswati III. The emblem of Hlane is the lion under whose name His Majesty is known in Siswati as "Ngwenyama". Lion were reintroduced to Swaziland after an absence of 30 years on 9th February 1994. This is a significant event for Swaziland, one of which the Nation can be very proud. The name "Hlane" means "wilderness" and has a special place in the Swazi Nation. It is here that great herds of game were to be found and in the sixties were almost depleted. His Majesty King Sobhuza II recognised the need for conservation. After seeing and supporting the creation of Mlilwane, the King appointed Ted Reilly to restore and protect the herds of Hlane, whose affairs to this day are personally governed by His Majesty. Now the National Hunt or "Butimba" rewards hunters with surplus stock from the regenerated herds.

Two young lionesses at Hlane. Photo courtesy of Big Game Parks

There is something magical about Hlane with its low shrubland, still heat and large tracts of dense bush. Large herds of zebra, kudu, wildebeest, nyala and impala roam the park. A herd of young elephant are frequently viewed close to the Ndlovu Camp; 22 elephants have been re-introduced into Hlane over the past 3 years.

A flock of young ostrich, stroll into the camp dancing and preening themselves. For the visitor who has little time in Swaziland, to observe and enjoy the wildlife, the variety of birds within the camp and the stillness of unspoilt Africa, is a great experience.

The natural mortality rate within Hlane attracts the scavengers. The Marabou storks nest each year in trees close to the Bhubesi camp. This is the most southerly nesting area in Africa and last year several chicks were born within the park. Vulture, jackals and hyenas are resident in Hlane and play their very important role in the ecology of the reserve. With the many other introductions of formerly exterminated game, Hlane's wildlife has grown dramatically. This is an unspoilt, underdeveloped area of Africa and visitors should make the time to spend a night or more here. Accommodation is extremely comfortable and the rangers are courteous and informed. By day if you wish to walk out of the spacious camp ground, you may easily hire the services of a game ranger to guide you.

Nhlovu Camp

2 fully furnished huts are situated close to a central "boma" and cooking area. One hut sleeps 8, it has 2 double rooms and a loft to accommodate 4 persons. The other hut sleeps 3; each is very well furnished in solid wood, with crockery, cutlery glasses and cooking utensils. Visitors must provide their own food as there is no shop in the Reserve, but each hut has a gas fridge for storage of fresh produce. The huts are equipped with bedding and towels and a wash basin is installed in the bedroom. Toilets and showers are located in the central ablution block. Lighting is by paraffin lamps and candles, so remember to bring a torch. Cooking is upon an open camp fire or on barbeques placed around the camp. Night sounds of warthogs, elephant and hyenas, accompany the smells of cooking and fire smoke.

Bhubesi Camp

The Bhubesi camp, 18 kms from the Ndlovu Camp is only 2 kms from the road. Three recently built lodges nestle above a gentle creek overlooking a riverine expanse of hardwood trees, sand and water.

The 3 lodges built of Hlane stone, are well furnished and fitted to a very high standard. The furniture is made by PS Woodwork, renowned for their original work which blends into the natural beauty of the camp. Each lodge will accommodate 4 persons in two separate bedrooms. There is a fully fitted bathroom and shower, separate toilet and a well equipped kitchen. Bhubesi has electricity, a stove and fridge in the kitchen and the welcoming lounge includes a Jetmaster fire for those cold riverside evenings. Summer days can be very hot; the Bhubesi lodges have a natural air-conditioning system which ensures that cool air enters the lodge throughout the day. Perhaps the best time is the evening when you sit in your own garden over the creek, and watch the vultures bathe in the Mbuluzana River below. Observe the hole-nesting birds such as glossy starlings and colourful kingfishers, see the crocodile slither over the sand into the water and be aware that you are sharing this sanctuary with the wildlife, an honoured guest amongst them.

Try to enjoy both camps at Hlane, as they offer completely different terrain and the opportunity to view dense bush life, riverine birds, mammals and flora.

Hlane Royal National Park, P.O. Box 234, Mbabane, Tel: 44541, Fax: 40957 a/h & weekends Tel: 61037,61591/2/3

Custom-designed furniture for your home and office

P.S. Woodwork (Pty) Ltd
P.O. Box 1483, Mbabane Tel: (268) 61239, 61817

Comfortable accommodation at Bhubesi Camp, Hlane, Photo courtesy of Big Game Parks

Leave Hlane Royal National Park heading south towards Manzini, approximately 20 kms on the left turn towards Siteki. Siteki, which means "Place of Marriage" is the only town on the Lubombo escarpment, it is set 2000 metres above sea level and on a clear day you may be fortunate to see the Indian Ocean from a viewing place close to Siteki. Previously known as "Stegi", this is the oldest town in the Kingdom, it was the customs office for Lourenco Marques (now Maputo).

MUTI-MUTI NATURE RESERVE

Located south of Siteki is the Muti-Muti Nature Reserve, a new conservation area established by Eco-Africa Safaris. From a high vantage point, on a clear day you can see the entire breadth of Swaziland to the west and across the floodplains of Mozambique in the east. A variety of different habitats occur within the reserve from the moist belt forests, the much treasured kiaat woodlands, rocky plateau and cliffs and open savannah. Over 250 bird species have already been identified and the rare Samango monkey choose Muti-Muti as his habitat.

THE SITEKI HOTEL

8 Rooms all with bath, resident's lounge and dining room.

The Siteki Hotel is one of the oldest hotels in the Kingdom and has a lot of charm. An oasis in the hot lowveld, the Siteki Hotel maintains its old world charm and character; the staff are attentive and the resident's lounge and dining room maintain their colonial appeal. There is a good table d'hote menu at night and simple meals are available during the day. Originally owned by Mrs Wigman Duke who came from Bournmouth, England to marry a Big Game Hunter, the game of tennis was introduced to Stegi by Mrs Wigman who personally ran the hotel for many years. Present proprietor Graham Duke has operated the Siteki Hotel for many years and he knows the immediate area intimately. Each guest is made extremely welcome at this country hotel. The dining room caters for Sunday lunch for visitors exploring the

SITEKI HOTEL

SWAZILAND

INDHLOVU KAYI KOHLWA

A small country hotel on the Lubombo mountain range

Phone 34126
PO Box 33, Siteki
Ideally situated for day visits to the Lowveld game sanctuaries

The Siteki Hotel

Lubombo and Muti Muti area. The Siteki Hotel is just off the newly tarred road and an ideal place for visitors entering Swaziland from Bordergate/Mananga post or through Lomahasha which borders with Mozambique enroute to Natal. This has become a very popular route over the past year and the Siteki Hotel is the ideal spot to stay awhile and enjoy the wonderful scenery and wildlife reserves of North East Swaziland. The terrain here is high and very beautiful with lush vegetation and the slightly tangy, salt smell of the distant Mozambique coast. From Siteki to Maputo is only 2 hours drive, this will be less once the new highway being built by Italian contractors is finished in 1995.
The Siteki Hotel, P.O. Box 33, Siteki, Tel: 34126

Return to the main road and travel the remaining 53 kms to Manzini. You will pass through low bush country and cross the railway line at Mpaka junction linking rail traffic between Swaziland, Mozambique and South Africa.

CIRCULAR DRIVE OF NORTH EAST SWAZILAND

A circular tour within the North East of Swaziland is to turn off right 8 kms before Hhelehhele at Mafutseni and pass through Mpisi, Luve, Mliba, Croydon to Balegane.
One of the old Swaziland families, the Buckhams, settled in the Croydon area which explorer William Buckham named after his birthplace - Croydon, London. In the 1890's the Buckham family became landowners in the village of Buckham which borders the Black Mbuluzi River and the family roots are still firmly planted in this area.
The road from Mafutseni to Mliba is now fully tarred and plans to extend this work west towards the Matsamo/Jeppes Reef border post are well in hand.
The road will bring you out onto the main road at Tshaneni when you can return to Manzini through the sugar estates, on a resurfaced road from Mananga/Bordergate post to the Mlawula railhead (which is used by the Sugar Estates) and past Hlane Royal National Park. The entire journey is 197 kms. Check the condition of the gravel road before embarking upon this route which will complete your knowledge of North East Swaziland.

Turgid river running high

Chapter 8

The North West of Swaziland

The Journey from Jeppes Reef/Matsamo to Mbabane	142
Protea Pigg's Peak Hotel	142
Coral Stephens Mohair	145
Phophonyane Lodge and Nature Reserve	145
Havelock	146
Pigg's Peak	146
Tintsaba Crafts	147
Malolotja Nature Reserve	148
Hawana Park	152
Ngwenya Iron Ore Mine	152

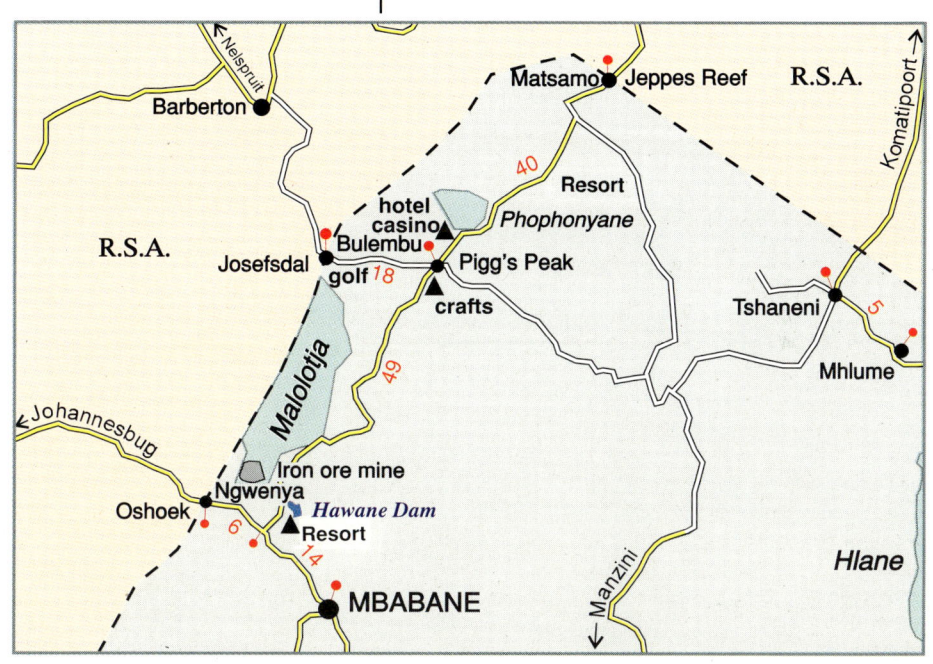

THE JOURNEY FROM JEPPES REEF/MATSAMO TO MBABANE

Visitors entering the Kingdom through the Jeppes Reef/Matsamo border (open 07h00 - 18h00) choose one of the most beautiful routes into Swaziland. This is the Highveld of the Kingdom, with its champagne air, rolling mountains covered in majestic indigenous growth, green pines and fragrant eucalyptus and breathtaking views. From the border to the capital are located the three highest peaks in Swaziland, the oldest iron ore mine in the world, spectacular waterfalls, bushmen paintings and ranges of hills which seem to stretch to eternity.

Travel 25 kms from the border and on the right is the entrance to the Protea Piggs Peak Hotel and Casino.

PROTEA PIGGS PEAK HOTEL AND CASINO

106 luxury rooms with ensuite bath, telephone, television with M-Net in each room, superb views from every balcony, Casino and large slots room, 5 Conference rooms with up to the minute equipment, 2 restaurants, regular live entertainment, horse stables, swimming pool, lawn bowls, putt putt green, 2 tennis courts, 2 squash courts. Secretarial services on request.

The Protea Piggs Peak Hotel is one of the best in the group, well appointed, wonderfully located and there is a very friendly and concerned manner about all of the staff as they tend to visitors' every wish and whim. This hotel is set in superb scenery high above the valleys beneath the Makonjwa Mountains. Designed to cater for visitors searching for the peace and beauty of the highlands, the Protea Piggs Peak Hotel meets the needs of nature lovers, sports enthusiasts, Casino experts and night owls. Each day is packed with lots to do or just nothing if you prefer. Top class restaurants, luxury bedrooms, a full casino and excellent sporting facilities, the Protea Pigg's Peak Hotel has just everything for everyone and each double bedroom has an individual balcony facing the mountains and valleys below.

Sports lovers can choose to play squash in air conditioned glass backed courts, tennis on 2 floodlit courts or bowls on the hotel green. There is a gymnasium for the energetic, a pool and relaxing sauna. The hotel has its own stables offering a range of riding trails and outrides into the surrounding hills and forests plus docile horses for beginners and children.

Within the Hotel is a boutique called "Tekwane" where the cream of the crop in crafts and handmade items can be found, Coral Stephen's mohair, tapestries, fashion and ethnic clothes, jewellery and ceramics. Sheila Freemantle, well informed upon Swazi handcraft often gives talks to hotel guests upon this aspect of Swazi culture.

The two restaurants, the top class Egumeni and the Forest cater for every taste from superb a la carte choice of world class dishes to curry evenings, carvery lunches, extensive buffets and intimate seafood suppers. Pianists play in each restaurant and table magic and ventriloquists add a little sparkle to the evening. Frequently special theme evenings are arranged for visiting groups.

The Casino and extensive Slots areas have been totally refurbished and extended. Guests can play Punto Banco, Roulette and Blackjack plus try their luck at the R1,000,000 Jackpot slot. Regular promotional weekends and evenings bring visitors from afar to win those extra few chips which make all the difference to a holiday.

Protea Piggs Peak Hotel and Casino, P.O.Box 385, Pigg's Peak, Tel: 71104/5, Telex 2024 WD, Fax: 71382, Toll free No: 0800-11-9000

Set in the beautiful mountainous highlands of north-west Swaziland. Five star accommodation and cuisine. Conference and sporting facilities.

Casino Enterprises (Pty) Ltd

PO Box 385, Piggs Peak,
Kingdom of Swaziland
Tel: (+268) 71104/5
Fax: (+268) 71382
Toll Free 0800-11-9000

Tekwane Shop

Glorious Highveld scenery

CORAL STEPHEN'S MOHAIR

Set below the peaks of North West Swaziland, a hand spinning and weaving of fine mohair industry has been operating for years. Coral Stephen's work may be seen at a number of retail outlets, most notably at "Living in Africa" in the Swazi Plaza, Mbabane, and in the shop within the Protea Pigg's Peak Hotel,"Tekwane". Coral Stephen's Mohair is world renowned amd exported to Europe and U.S.A. Visitors wishing to visit should telephone first.
Coral Stephens, Tel: 71140

PHOPHONYANE LODGE AND NATURE RESERVE

Travel a further 3 kms from the Protea Pigg's Peak Hotel and on the right you will see a sign to the Phophonyane Lodge and Nature Reserve. The distinctive sign depicting a colourful bird is outstanding in daylight, slow down, to spot it after dark. At this point, you are only 63 kms from Mbabane. Deep within the natural beauty of cascading water, soaring mountains and indigenous forest lies this beautiful reserve which is serviced by double - storied thatched cottages, a honeymoon suite and an exclusive luxury tented camp. Only twenty three people can be accomodated in 3 separate camps offering a high degree of privacy. All units are self-contained but an a la carte, licensed restaurant is available to those not wishing to cater for themselves. For the visitor who is seeking peace, seclusion and scenic splendour, Phophonyane is a wonderful choice. The nature lover will find an extraordinary variety of habitats in a relatively small area, an exciting variety of birds, flora and the small game species of the forest. This is a hide-away place to be enjoyed.

Phophonyane has landscaped gardens filled with flowering shrubs and each lodge has its own private area of garden. The owner, Rod de Vletter is a fund of knowledge upon the flora and birdlife within the reserve. He and his wife Lungile, have created a natural swimming pool, capturing the waters from the Phophonyane Falls into a series of canals which spill into a pool above the river Phophonyane. This is crystal clear, bilharzia free water, wonderful to enjoy after a long walk along the riverine paths. A number of trails meander through the reserve to view points above and below the falls and to natural pools set within the forests.

The lodges sleep 5, they are tastefully furnished and equipped to the last detail. Each has a self contained kitchen with electric stove and refrigerator, a bathroom with shower, handbasin and toilet. The lounge is comfortably furnished, open log fires greet you in winter when dinner can be served in your lodge.

Luxury tented camps situated next to the Falls will sleep groups of 6 and may well suit

View across the main Piggs Peak road

Phophonyane Lodge

LUXURY ACCOMMODATION IN DOUBLE STOREY THATCHED COTTAGES AND THE TOP COTTAGE OR EXCLUSIVE TENTED CAMP. WE NOW ALSO OFFER ADDITIONAL LUXURY ACCOMMODATION AT BETSAMOYA COTTAGE, SITUATED ON ITS OWN NATURE RESERVE 5 KMS AWAY. ALL UNITS ARE SELF CONTAINED, A-LA-CARTE LICENSED RESTAURANT, BAR WITH BALCONEY OVER-LOOKING THE RIVER. PRIVATE NATURE RESERVE WITH SPECTACULAR GARDENS AND NATURAL LANDSCAPE, INDIGENOUS FOREST, BIRDLIFE, WALKING AND SWIMMING, EASY ACCESS TO KRUGER PARK, SELF GUIDED SCENIC DAY TOURS CAN BE UNDERTAKEN IN SURROUNDING AREAS.

WRITE TO P.O. BOX 199, PIGG'S PEAK FOR BROCHURE OR PHONE DIRECT (268) 71319/ 71429 * FAX (268) 71319, MBABANE OFFICE PHONE (268) 45006 * FAX (268) 44246 *

Swimming in a rock pool at Phophonyane, Photo by Rod de Vletter

young families seeking open air experience. Further developments at Phophonyane include a new bar with balcony overlooking the river; a great way to enjoy sundowners and evening dinner. The new Betsamoya Nature Reserve, just 5 kms from Phophonyane covers a large area of North Western Swaziland ,at present in a virgin state, with some wildlife, the Reserve contains a self contained cottage which sleeps 5,adding to the superb facilities already in place at Phophonyane. The tranquillity and beauty of Phophonyane Reserve is breathtaking; this is Swaziland at its natural best. In 1995, 89 hectares are to be added to the reserve enhancing the roaming and self guiding areas for visitors to enjoy.

From here you are well placed to explore some of the most remote and mysterious parts of the country, Swaziland's other nature reserves or the new reserves of KaNgwane. Rod de Vletter is working on the establishment of an International Nature Reserve which will encompass parts of Swaziland, Zululand, KaNgwane and Mozambique. This is a very ambitious enterprise which is receiving serious attention from various governments.

Phophonyane Lodge and Nature Reserve, P.O. Box 199, Pigg's Peak,
Tel: 71319, 71429, 45006, Fax: 71319 & 44246.

Leave Phophonyane Nature Reserve and return to the main road, turn right and continue towards Pigg's Peak. You will cross a 3 way junction. To the left is a wonderfully scenic route towards Endzingeni, Balegane and Tshaneni or to Croydon, Mliba, Luve, Mpisi and Mafutseni which joins the main Manzini to Siteki road. For the more intrepid traveller in a robust vehicle, this is a magnificent route dropping form the Highveld of Pigg's Peak to the middleveld at Balegane and Mpisi, finally to the lowveld where you may wish to continue to the Nature reserves of Hlane, Mkhaya and Mlawula. A circular trip encompassing a turnoff left, 6 kms from the Jeppes Reef border, which takes you through Herefords, across the Mzimmene River and right towards Endzingeni and Pigg's Peak, is very rewarding; the entire circular journey is 80 kms. Be sure to enquire as to the condition of the road prior to setting out, especially in the rainy summer months.

A further kilometre towards Pigg's Peak brings you to a turning right which is a gravel road covering 19 kms to the village of Havelock.

HAVELOCK

Havelock was named after Sir Arthur Havelock who was a Governor of Natal. Two gold prospectors who obtained a concession at Havelock in 1886 named the area Havelock where Bulembu Asbestos Mine is now located. The mining village has an excellent sporting club with a 9 hole golf club, squash, tennis and bowls facilities.

The route to Havelock is very beautiful and to enjoy a picnic or braai at the end of the drive makes the journey very worthwhile. As Havelock is only 1 km from the Bulembu/Josefsdal border post, (OPEN 08h00 - 16h00) this is a wonderful day out for visitors from the Eastern Transvaal or beyond.

Return to the main road between Jeppes Reef/Matsamo and Pigg's Peak and turn right towards Piggs Peak and Mbabane.

PIGGS PEAK

Piggs Peak was named after William Pigg, an early prospector who found a gold reef here. Originally, the ore was trammed to stamp batteries just below the falls. Between 1889 and 1954, when the mine ceased operations, 119,235 ounces of gold were produced but it was never considered to be a spectacular find. William Pigg left the village which was named after him and settled in Natal next to a family called "Hogg"; one of his sons is said to have married a daughter of this Hogg family. Another local prospector named Andy Burnett recovered a fortune in gold which attracted offers of marriage from interested women. Irritated with continuous intrusions, Burnett blew up the entrance to the mine and left. His fortune was soon dissipated and Burnett returned to work as a carpenter at the Piggs Peak Gold Mine. He could not relocate the entrance to his old gold mine and was furious when the entire area was covered with Pine trees, camouflaging possible sites for prospecting. Piggs Peak is now reliant upon timber and the byproducts of the forests.

Pass through the town and on the left stop at Tintsaba Crafts located within the Highlands Inn.

Rafting down the Nkomati River.
Photo by Rod de Vletter

Tintsaba Crafts at Highlands Inn, Piggs Peak

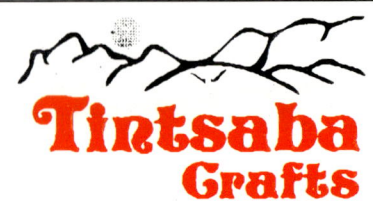

Piggs Peak
Box 340

Sisal weaving in baskets
and jewellery
Unique items from
Northern Swaziland.

Open 7 days a week.

at
Piggs Peak Hotel & Casino

Visit our attractive shop &
see the cream of Swazi crafts
& interesting African pieces
& clothes

Open every day

TINTSABA CRAFTS

Sheila Freemantle works with groups of rural women who make sisal baskets, beadwork, grass baskets, sleeping mats and mountain grass basketware. Regular workshops are held to encourage awareness of the environment and the importance of precious grasses and trees within the rural areas. Sheila encourages the use of non-rare woods to safeguard the endangered kiatt tree. Wooden baskets made from the indigenous acacia are brought to Tintsaba Crafts together with creeper basket. Tintsaba is ethnic in image and encourages rural craft development on a non-profit making basis. Groups of women specialising in sisal products, river and mountain grasses are frequently met and encouraged to produce quality work. The making of baskets is an age old industry as many are for practical purposes; carrying of maize, vegetables and wood and as eating utensils. The highly decorative baskets made by the Swazi women are in constant demand, they are individual to each basketmaker and reflect the cultural background of this land. Grasses are seasonal, the mountain grass is harvested in February whereas, the familar Sisal is a year round material. The Komati carvers are Swaziland's oldest craft centre, the groups have difficulty in obtaining kiaat and soapstone and should hold a permit from their chief to cut the scarce kiaat. Many chiefs are extremely watchful of the environment and this care needs to be imparted to the carvers. They are urged to plant the branches to regenerate the wood and encouraged to supplement with less endangered woods. Handcraft include sleeping and plaited mats, soapstone carvings, clay pots, calabashes, beer strainers and beadwork; all of these may be found from time to time at Tintsaba Crafts. An interesting traditional item is the "Swazi Loveletter" made from a

View North of Gobolondlo. Photo by Rod de Vletter

MALOLOTJA NATURE RESERVE
SWAZILAND NATIONAL TRUST COMMISSION

Variety of wild game
Trail network for 1 to 7 days hikes
Log cabins- fully furnished
Camping and caravan facilities
25km game viewing roads
Trout fishing
Magnificent mountain scenery
Peace and tranquility
Sailing at Hawane Nature Reserve

For enquiries contact
The Senior Warden, P.O. Box 1797, Mbabane, Swaziland
Tel: (268) 43060 Bookings: P.O. Box 100, Lobamba. Tel: (268) 61178/9 Fax: 61875

wildebeest tail, covered in beads, the "head" of the figurine has a top knot and a necklace of beads. These are made by Swazi maidens and presented to the menfolk of their choice to be worn at his waist.
Tintsaba Crafts, P.O. Box 340, Piggs Peak, Tel: 71260, Tekwane, Tel: 71104
Leave Tintsaba Crafts and continue on the main tar road to Mbabane. 35 kms along this very spectacular route you will arrive at Malolotja Nature Reserve on the right.

MALOLOTJA NATURE RESERVE

Malolotja Nature Reserve, the responsibility of The Swaziland National Trust Commission, is approximately 18,000 hectares of highveld and middleveld landscape. It contains two of Swaziland's highest mountains, Ngwenya and Silotwana plus the highest waterfalls, the Malolotja Falls which are 95m. The altitude ranges from 1900m to 650m and houses a tremendous variety of plants, reptiles and geographical complexities. Broken mountain peaks, lush valleys, plains and deep river gorges, waterfalls and potholes are all present here. There are 200 kms of hiking trails ranging from easy walks to fairly strenuous climbs. Only one group of backpackers may stay in one of the 17 camps at any one time and the sites are small with space for only one or two tents.

Birdlife includes the blue swallow, bald ibis, blue crane and flufftails. The impressive jackal buzzard and the secretary bird occur in Malolotja as does the rare sacred ibis and in the impressive protea woodland, the rare Gurney's sugarbird has been sighted. This is a bird spotters paradise; several forest species live in the mistbelt area of Malolotja: the Knysna lourie, chorister robin, crowned eagle, grey cuckoo shrike and the rare narina trogon. Reptiles number 26 species counted to date, include the puff adder, boomslang and Mozambique spitting cobra. Game viewing can be good and you may spot blesbok, blue wildebeest, zebra and the red hartebeest.

The geology of the reserve is particularly interesting as it incorporates the oldest sedimentary rocks in the world containing the fossils of blue-green algae estimated to be 3.5 billion years old and part of the Barberton greenstone belt. At the southern end of Malolotja is an area rich in ironstone mined by Stone Aged people for the red pigment and more recently for the metal content.

Possibly one of the greatest attractions is the superb variety of wild flowers. Walking along the lower hilltops, valley and riverine areas, the visitor will see a magnificent selection including the Barberton and Kaapsehoop cycads and proteas which attract the sunbirds and sugarbirds.

Accommodation is excellent; 5 fully equipped log cabins will sleep a maximum of 6 persons. Remember to bring your own bedding, towels and provisions. Each lodge has two double bedrooms, a kitchen with its own stove and fridge, a lounge, dining room complete with an open log fireplace and separate bathroom and toilet. Camping and caravanning sites are placed within the Reserve and visitors should pack a warm jersey or jacket as this Highveld nature spot can become chilly in the evenings. Visitors please note there is no shop within the reserve, the closest petrol garage is 20 kms away and wood for your fire may be purchased from the main office. Trout fishing is available from 2 dams within the reserve. Licences may be obtained for fly fishing all year round from the main office.
Malolotja Nature Reserve, P.O. Box 100 Lobamba, Tel: 61178/9, Fax: 61875

SWAZILAND ROYAL INSURANCE CORPORATION

Find us at our
headquarters building
Lilunga House,
Gilfillan Street, Mbabane
and at the New Mall,
Mbabane.

P.O. Box 917, Mbabane
Tel: (+ 268) 43231/9
Tel Ad: "Insurance"
Telex: 2043 WD
Fax: (+268) 46415

INSURERS TO THE NATION

Leave the reserve and travel towards Mbabane, on the left you will see the Hawane Dam which is used by birdwatchers, and for board sailing, canoeing and dinghies. Interested visitors should enquire from Malolotja Nature Reserve.

HAWANA PARK

Situated next to the Hawane Dam is a new resort placed on the rolling hills overlooking the dam and the valleys towards Mbabane and distant Lubombo. Still in its early stages, Hawana Park is creating log cabins, caravan parking areas and a especially secluded place for tents. This is a wonderful area to discover on foot or horseback: outrides over the hills towards Mbabane or Ngwenya can be arranged from the nearby Hawane Stables and the area is full of interest for ramblers and gentle walkers. Wild flowers and birdlife abound, visit this serene spot and forget about the hustle and bustle of life. Within a few kilometres is the entrance gate to Hawane Dam Nature Reserve - park your car and for a small charge visit the dam and enjoy the bird life.

Malolotja Nature Reserve is within 10 kms of Hawana Park, entrance charges are reasonable and the possibilities within the park are numerous. Walking trails, bird watching, wild flower identification and of course enjoyment of the spectacular scenery and abundant fauna are all here, so close to Hawana Park.

Accomodation is in 2 bedded chalets, with sleeper couches for children, fully equipped; just bring your food and drink An ablution block will service the caravan and tented areas, whilst the chalets have their own ensuite bathrooms.

Hawana Park, P.O. Box 4886, Mbabane, Tel: (+268) 46416, 44522 Fax: (+268) 42485, 43318

HAWANA PARK

Fully equipped and Chalets, facing the Dam and the beautiful valley below.

Secluded and private Camping and Caravan sites will be available at a later stage at the most affordable rates.

Hawana Dam Nature Reserve and Malolotja Nature Reserve are a short drive away.

Only 9 Kms from Ngwenya/Oshoek Border, only 15 kms from Mbabane
(No Need to Negotiate the Malagwane Hill)

CENTRAL RESERVATIONS
PO Box 4886, Mbabane, Kingdom of Swaziland
Tel: (+268) 46416, 44522   Fax: (+268) 42485, 43318

THE NGWENYA IRON ORE MINE

Part of the South Western area of Malolotja contains Ngwenya mountain peak. Beneath this peak are a series of caves and workings which date back to 41 000 BC when haematite and specularite were sought for cosmetic and ritual requirements. The primitive miners confined their work to the summit of the mountain as they feared the presence of the great horned snake (god of the underworld who lived in the heart of the mountain). There is a warden at the gates of Ngwenya so that visitors may go direct to the Mine on certain days of the week, alternatively, you request a guide from Malolotja who will accompany you to the gate and to view the vast open pit which marked the modern workings of the Ngwenya Iron Ore Mine, no longer in operation. The vastness of this area is amazing, travel towards the deep pool which falls fathoms beneath ground surface, climb above the pit towards the ancient Lion Cavern which is a tiny man made pit rendolent with ancient history. Look across the foothills towards the Eastern Transvaal; further exploration takes you to the abandoned office, workshops and plant of the recent Iron Ore Company.

Your guide will also take you to the Forbes Reef Gold Mine which is no longer in operation. You may enter the old workings with a guide. Unfortunately, the previous Forbes reef "Ghost Town" has practically disappeared.

You have now completed the entire area of the Kingdom of Swaziland. We hope you have enjoyed the experience of this land and its people and we all hope you will visit us again very soon.

The following chapter deals with the immediate surrounding areas of tourist interest which you may wish to see in conjunction with your exploration of the Kingdom of Swaziland.

The Ngwenya Iron Ore Mine workings

THE
ELEGANCE AND GRACE...

...Still lives on. Step in the grand-new Polana situated in the heart of coastal Africa with a hint of something tropical. There's a host of passionate people — all with their individual role of excellence to play — to pamper — to placate your every need.

THE POLANA, THE PLACE TO REMEMBER, THE PLACE TO BE SPOILED.

Polana

A BETTER EXCELLENCE OF LIFE.

Ave. Julius Nyerere, 1380, Maputo, Moçambique Telefone 491001/7 Fax 491480 Telex 6-278 POLAN MO

★★★★★

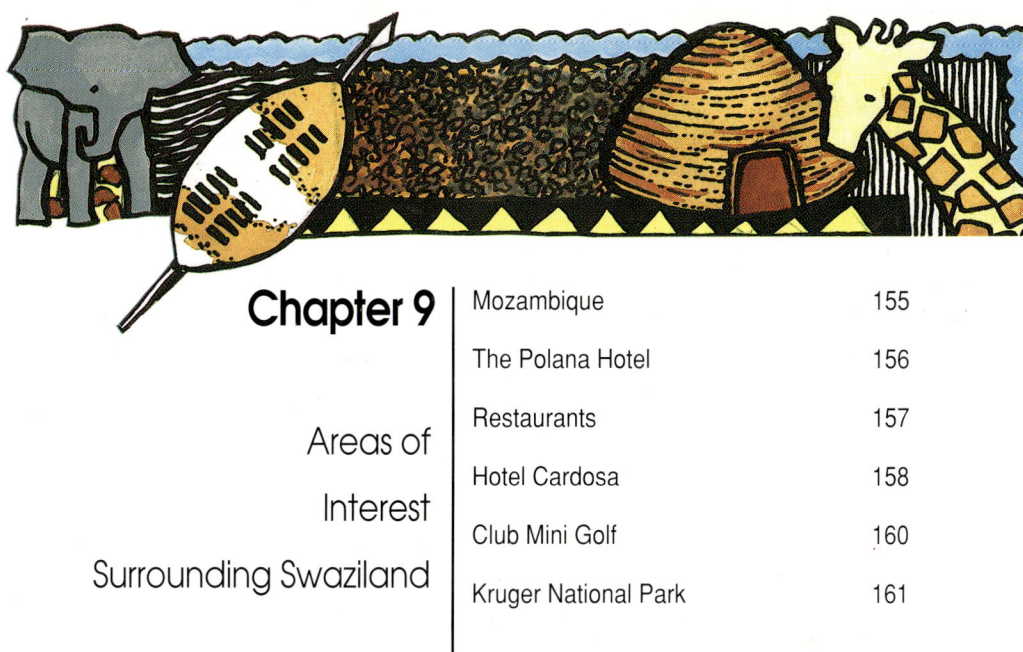

Chapter 9

Areas of Interest Surrounding Swaziland

Mozambique	155
The Polana Hotel	156
Restaurants	157
Hotel Cardosa	158
Club Mini Golf	160
Kruger National Park	161

MOZAMBIQUE

The country of Mozambique lies to the East of Swaziland, just over the Lubombo Mountains. The history of the two countries is intertwined and close links have been maintained before and after the changes from colonial rule to independence. Trade flourishes through Maputo harbour, the closest seaport to Swaziland, via the railway line which enters Mozambique at Goba, east of Mlawula Station. The port of Maputo increasingly handles exports and imports from and to Swaziland and Southern Africa.

From Swaziland you can fly direct to Maputo using the Mozambique National Airline, Lineas Aereas de Mozambique or Royal Swazi National Airways. The flight takes 30 minutes from Matsapha and visas are necessary, these can be obtained from the Mozambique Embassy in Mbabane, usually within a week, although issue can be arranged in 2 days if necesssary. Many people now drive to Maputo crossing at Lomahasha, (07h00 - 16h45) the journey from Mbabane to Maputo currently takes about 4 hours. The road between Namaacha and Maputo is poor although major reconstruction is underway and will be finished in 1995. You will need to take your vehicle's papers with you and to pay for insurance and documentation at the border before entering Mozambique or book a tour with Umhlanga Tours. The scenery is breathtaking across the Lobombo mountains and a first stop at the Hotel Libombas in Namaacha for breakfast, lunch or to stay overnight is well worthwhile, as the border closes early in the evening, this is a popular hotel for overnight stops either way.

Customs are fairly strict, it is wise to declare every item you are carrying and you must register your foreign currency upon arrival. Duty free allowances includes 2 litres of spirits, 5 litres of wine and 200 cigarettes. Duty is payable on craft items bought in

Mozambique and taken out of the country.

There are taxis from the airport although the major hotels offer a transfer service for guests. Alternatively you may rent a car from either Avis or Hertz who have offices at the airport.

Maputo is a sprawling, fascinating city, there is a holiday atmosphere about the capital, its tropical climate, sea breezes, red tiled Colonial buildings, ships gently sliding into harbour, the unhurried pace of life and the ever cheerful expressions of its people all contribute to "a forget about the rest of the world" feeling. The central market sells some interesting and skilfully made curios at inexpensive prices and despite shortages, the Mozambican people smile and are happy to welcome visitors. This is a country coming back to life which needs encouragement from enquiring and interested tourists.

THE POLANA HOTEL

169 rooms ensuite, 20 suites, central air conditioning, telephone, TV and satellite channels, swimming pool, tennis court, 2 restaurants and bars, gymnasium, delicatessen, Salon de The, superb restaurant, Conference facilities for 250 persons.

The Polano Hotel is the premier hotel in Maputo and Mozambique, it has been beautifully renovated and refurbished to a very high standard, restoring this Colonial style hotel to a level of luxury rarely found in Southern Africa. Every bedroom is magnificently furnished, the decor is subtle, restful and charming. Large rooms with big windows recall a bygone era when time was less strenuous and life travelled at a slower pace. Every Polana staff member is trained to a professional standard, dressed in their distinctive hotel uniforms, they make your stay a completely memorable experience. Magnificent public rooms, an initmate salon de thé, a light and bright restaurant and a discreet bar which serves a wide selection of exotic cocktails, make this top class hotel the only choice for many visitors. There is so much to see and do here and the oasis of the Polana is a fantastic respite after a busy day.

The Polana Hotel, 1380, Julius Nyerere Ave, Maputo,
Tel: (258) (1) 491001/7, Fax: (258) (1) 491480, Telex: 6278 POLAN MO.

Swimming pool at the Polana Hotel

The Polana Salon de Thé

Maputo is alive with activity, since the election, the whole country has responded to progress and is pushing ahead towards a gradual economic independence. The successsful election at the end of 1994 is a source of joy to most residents of Mozambique who wish to rebuild their lives. The United Nations personnel who were in the country to oversee the elections are due to leave in early 1995 and tourism is now a more vibrant facet of the economy. Hotels are opening up, other parts of Mozambique are now frequently visited for their beaches and fishing. Beira, the coastal town further north has a number of hotels and a few restaurants which are proving popular to local residents and visitors. The other coastal villages are developing; small resorts, hotels, camping areas and some wonderful swimming, snorkeling and fishing is now freely available to the adventurous visitor.

Restaurants in Maputo have a lot to offer, the wonderful choice of Mozambican prawns and of course peri-peri chicken which every tourist wants to try. However, there are a number of excellent top quality restaurants offering Chinese, Continental and Indian dishes which must be visited.

Crafts are also on the increase, the main market in central Maputo contains not only fruit, vegetable, fish, meat and spice merchants but a section of crafts ranging from wooden carvings in hard and soft woods, baskets and bead work. Some of the carving is excellent such as the boxes which fit inside each other, the delicately carved tables and chairs and the sensitive African head carvings. Paintings are also here in vibrant oranges, reds and greens,

The Portuguese tradiiton of sitting at pavement cafes and watching the world pass by has returned to the cities of Mozambique, a very welcome return which most visitors enjoy, this coupled with a cold beer or glass of wine and those tasty snacks certainly help the day pass very gently before going on to the disco's and dance places in the evening.

MOZAMBIQUE PORTS AND RAILWAYS
EMPRESA NACIONAL DE PORTOS E CAMINHOS DE FERRO DE MOCAMBIQUE E.E.

If you look at the map of Southern Africa it becomes abundantly obvious that Mozambique ports are the natural choice to move goods in and out of Southern Africa. Mozambique's close proximity to the main and rapidly expanding markets of Southern Africa provide substantial savings in cost and time.

MOZAMBIQUE PORTS AND RAILWAYS
Dhlan'ubeka House, Walker Street, PO Box 1873, MBABANE, Swaziland
Tel: (+268) 43285 (off) (+268) 43474 (Res) Fax: (+268) 43803, Telex 2251 CFMWD

THE HOTEL CARDOSO

131 ensuite bedrooms, 6 large suites, 4 mini-suites, satellite TV, swimming pool, 2 restaurants, Al fresco entertainment area, cocktail bar overlooking the sea, coffee salon, Conference facilities, secretarial and business services.

The newly refurbished, splendid Hotel Cardoso has maintained its colonial, Portuguese charm, yet a new aura of colour, light and up to the minute facilities make this hotel a focal point in Maputo. The magnificent wooden staircase remains surrounded by spacious reception rooms. This is the gracious hotel of a bygone era offering a charming new restaurant furnished in cane with soft green and tan textiles following a tropical bird theme. The room has ceiling fans and airconditioning and the selection of dishes is varied and excellent. There is a Salon de Café facing the street, this is the place to linger and enjoy the passing parade.

Perhaps the cocktail bar overlooking the swimming pool, the Maputo Bay, City Centre and Catembe Island is the fulcrum of the Cardoso, here one can sip an exciting cocktail from a frosted glass and watch the ships pass in the distance and the sun set over the estuary.

All of the bedrooms are furnished to a very high standard and the suites are spacious with private verandahs, luxury bathrooms and first class service.

The Hotel Cardoso caters especially for the business community with modern conference and seminar facilities, secretarial services and of course luxury accommodation for delegates.

This is an hotel which encourages the work weary to come to Maputo where the Indian ocean beckons,the Portuguese food entices and the Cardoso will pander to the visitor's every wish.

Transport to and from the airport will be provided by the hotel in chauffeur driven luxury bus and air and hotel packages can be arranged.

Hotel Cardoso, 707, Martires de Mueda Avenue, P.O. Box 35, Maputo, Mozambique, Tel: (258) (1) 49-1071/5, Fax: (258) (1) 49-1804 , Telex: 6029 Hocar

Sunset from the Hotel Cardoso

The Salon de Café at the Hotel Cardoso

HOTEL CARDOSO
The place for international businessmen

707, MARTIRES DE MUEDA AVE.
MAPUTO, MOZAMBIQUE
TEL: ++258-1-491071/5
FAX: ++258-1-491804

Fully Refurbished,
Luxury Suites,
Gracious Decor,
Superb Venue.

Please phone info Desk
Tel: (258 1) 490028

A LONRHO
de MOÇAMBIQUE
HOTEL

"Hotel Cardoso"
Maputo

RESTAURANTE ESPLANADA
DISCOTECA
PISCINA
GINÁSIO

Mini Golf

* Mini Golf Putt-Putt
* Restaurant and Karaoke Bar
* Gymnasium
* Swimming Pool
* The Best Night Club Scene in Maputo
* Disco

Action throughout the week..
The In-Place in fact the ONLY place in Maputo on Friday and Saturday Nights.

Complexo Mini Golf
Telelephone (+258) 1 490 382
Fax: (+258) 490 859
Av. Marginal No. 36
Maputo, Mozambique

COMPLEXO MINI GOLF

Located on the Avenue Marginal and facing the seafront is an exciting venue called the Club Mini-Golf. During the day this resort offers a Mini Putt Putt Golf course, a fully equipped gymnasium and wonderful, large swimming pool with grass lounging area. The Complexo Mini Golf is a great attraction to visitors to and residents of Maputo; at night the Karaoke bar swings into action with frequest live band attractions and a first class restaurant to encourage diners to stay. The Disco is the place to be most evenings but especially on Friday and Saturday nights. A large covered area is designated for the Mini Golf Disco with raised stage area for the disco DJ, dancers, bands or music groups. The music is loud, vibrant and exciting, the lights searching and the company is energetic and full of fun. Visitors to Maputo must make one night at the Complexo Mini Golf and return the following day for a relaxing game of putt putt or a swim.

Complexo Mini Golf, Ave Marginal 36, Maputo, Tel: (258) 1 490382, Fax: (258) 1 490859

Playing putt putt at the Mini Golf

Well equipped Gym at the Mini Golf

KRUGER NATIONAL PARK

Covering 200 million hectares of land in north and eastern Transvaal, the Kruger National Park is very close to the borders of Swaziland. From the Matsama/Jeppes Reef border post to the Malalane Gate is only 40 kms. Visitors may tour with Umhlanga Tours & Safaris (Tel: 46416) or take their own cars for one day trips or longer. The Kruger National Park is bounded by the Limpopo and Crocodile rivers and altitudes range from 900m to 200m. The variety of flora is wonderful from the tough mopane in the north and east of the park, home of the elephant and roan antelope, to the riverine forests of ironwod, mahogany and ebony. The almost prehistoric shape of the baobab tree which skirts the Limpopo contrasts with the red and elephant grasses and the marula trees which grow south of the Olifants river. This is the largest African game sanctuary, home to over 8,000 elephant, 26,000 buffalo, lion, cheetah, black and white rhino and hippo plus a multitude of buck species and flocks of birdlife. Accommodation is in 16 rest camps with cottages, thatched huts and camping facilities.

THE ZULULAND PARKS

Nduma Game Reserve
The closest game park to southern Swaziland is on the Mozambique border. The flood plains attract a vast variety of birdlife, fish and animal species resident in cycads, palms, wild orchids and impala lillies. Crocodile, hippo, nyala, cheetah, zebra and rhino live here with water fowl such as heron, fishing owl, barbet and broadbill. Accommodation is in 3 bedded rest huts with separate bathroom facilities.

Mkuzu Game Reserve
Close to Pongola the Mkuzu Game Reserve stands against the Lubombo Mountains and is bounded by the Mkuzi river. This is the land of fever trees, sycamore figs and knobthorns. There are 3 hides to view giraffe, impala, kudu, jackal, leopard, hippo and crocodile. The rest camp contains 2,4 and 6 bedded bungalows and cottages plus camping facilities.

Hluhluwe Game Reserve
280 kilometres north of Durban is the Hluhluwe Game Reserve which is one of the oldest wildlife sanctuaries in Africa. Less than 6% of the size of Kruger National Park, Hluhluwe contains a variety of forest, woodland, savannah and grassland species. This park is famous for its black and white rhino and re-introduced elephant. The camp includes 6 bedded cottages or rest huts.

Eastern Transvaal
Within the immediate vicinity of Swaziland are the towns of Barberton, Nelspruit, White River, Hazeyview and a little further away Graskop, Pilgrims Rest and Blyde River Canyon. The area is steeped in history as the old gold mines were established in the Barberton green hills and at Pilgrims Rest. Take time to visit the museum and Belhaven in Barberton and "Gods Window" which overlooks the Blyde River Canyon.

Herd of Buffalo in Kruger National Park

BIBLIOGRAPHY

Africa, South of the Sahara,1987, London: Europa Publications.
Barclays Business Guide to Swaziland, 1989, Barclays Bank of Swaziland Ltd.
Bonner, P. Kings, Commoners & Concessonaries, 1983, Cambridge : University Press.
Booth, A.R. Swaziland, Tradition and Change in a Southern African Kingdom,1983 , Westview Press: Colorado.
Forsyth-Thompson, C. Swaziland Business Year Book, 1994, Christina Forsyth-Thompson: Mbabane.
Grotpeter, J.J. Historical Dictionary of Swaziland, 1975, Scarecrow Press: New York.
Kuper, H. The Swazi - A South African Kingdom, 1963, New York: Holt, Rinehart & Winston Inc.
Levy, Jaynee. The Complete Guide to walks and Travels in Southern Africa, 1987, Struik: Cape Town.
Matsebula, Dr. J.M.S. A History of Swaziland, 3rd Edition, 1988, Longman: Cape Town.
Nxumalo, S.S. Our Swazi Way of Life, Mbabane: Swaziland Publishing and Printing.
SARTOC, A series of Swaziland brochures, Lorton Communications: Johannesburg
Satour, Our world of Wildlife, South Africa on Safari, 1989 ,Cape Town: Creda Press.
Strategic Options for Development of Swaziland, 1993, Prof. C.L. Jenkins,
World Tourism Organization: Madrid.
Swaziland for Everyone, 1993, Report for Hotels & Tourism Association of Swaziland, Motivational Marketing: Johannesburg.
Swaziland - The Royal Experience, 1993, Ministry of Broadcasting, Information and Tourism, Mbabane: E.C. Integrated Trade and Services Development Programme.
Scutt Joan, The Story of Swaziland,1984, Websters: Mbabane.
Time Out, Mozambique, December 1994, Editorial Economia: Maputo
Winchester-Gould, G.A. The Guide to Swaziland, 1978, Winchester Press: Johannesburg.

Further copies of the Swaziland Jumbo Tourist Guide are available at all leading Bookstores, Hotels and Tourist Shops in the Kingdom, or please write direct to the Publishers: R.O. Hussey & Company (Pty) Ltd, P.O. Box A225, Swazi Plaza, Mbabane, Kingdom of Swaziland, Tel: 46416, 44522, Fax: 42485, enclosing E20 or equivalent.

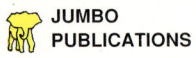

HOTELS, RESORTS, NATURE RESERVES & REST CAMPS

Assegai Inn
Prince Arthur Street, Hlathikhulu
Tel: (268) 76126

Lugogo Sun Hotel
Ezulwini Valley
Tel: (268) 61101, 61550   Fax: 61111
See display advert page 6

City Inn
Allister Miller Street
Tel: (268) 42406, 42034
See display advert page 56

Malolotja Nature Reserve
P.O. Box 100, Lobamba
Tel:(268) 61178/9   Fax: (268) 61875
See display advert page 149

Ezulwini Sun Hotel
Ezulwini Valley
Tel: (+268) 61201 Fax: (268) 61782
See display advert page 6

Mantenga Lodge
Ezulwini, Kingdom of Swaziland
Tel: (268) 61049   Fax: 61049
See display advert page 86

Forester's Arms Hotel
Tel: (268) 26084, 45707, 74177, 74377
Fax: (268) 74051
See display advert page 113

Meikles Mount
P.O. Box 13, Mhlambanyatsi
Tel: (268) 74110
See display advert page 114

Happy Valley Motel
Tel: (268) 61061, 61199, 61898,
61916, 61939   Fax: (268) 61050
See display advert page 87

Mgenule Motel
Ezulwini Valley.
Tel: (+268) 61041 / 2
See display advert page 72

Hawana Park
Near Ngwenya / Oshoek Border gate
Tel: (268) 46207 Fax: (268) 46207
See display advert page 152

Mkhaya Game Reserve
Tel: (268) 44541, 48613/4 Fax: (268) 40957
A/H & weekends: (268) 61037, 61591/2/3
See display advert I.F.C.

Highlands Inn
at Piggs Peak
P.O. Box 12, Piggs Peak
Tel: (268) 71144

Mlawula Nature Reserve
Tel: (268) 38885
Bookings: (268) 61178/9. Fax: (268) 61875
See display advert page 135

Hlane Royal National Park
Tel: (268) 44541, 48613/4 Fax: (268) 40957
A/H & weekends: (268) 61037, 61591/2/3
See display advert I.F.C.

Mlilwane Wildlife Sanctuary
Tel: (268) 44541, 48613/4 Fax: (268) 40957
A/H & weekends: (268) 61037, 61591/2/3
See display advert I.F.C.

Impala Arms Hotel
at Tshaneni
P.O. Box 34, Tshaneni
Tel: (268) 31244 Fax: (+268) 31045

Mocambique Hotel
Mahleka Street (Opposite the bus rank)
Tel: (268) 52489, 52586 Fax: 54044
See display advert page 106

Lavumisa Hotel
at Lavumisa

Tel: (268) (LAA) 7

Mountain Inn
Tel: (268) 42781   Fax: (268) 45393
Telex: 2135 WD
See display advert page 68

HOTELS, RESORTS, NATURE RESERVES & REST CAMPS

Muti Muti Nature Reserve
Near Siteki
Tel: (268) 71319/ 71429 Fax: (268) 71319

Siteki Hotel
P.O. Box 33, Siteki, Swaziland
Tel: (268) 34126
See display advert page 139

The New Bend Inn Hotel
P.O. Box 37, Big Bend, Swaziland
Tel: (+268) 36111/2 Fax (+268) 36364
See display advert page 120

Royal Swazi Sun Hotel
Tel: (268) 61001 Fax: 61606, 61128
See display advert page 6

The New George Hotel
Tel: (268) 52061 Fax: (268) 52061
Telex: 2071 WD
See display advert page 107

Smokey Mountain Village
Tel: (+268) 61291 / 61293
Fax: (+268) 46465
See display advert page 83

Nhlangano Sun Hotel & Casino
at Nhlangano
Tel: (268) 78211   Fax: (268) 78402
See display advert page 6

Swazi Inn
Tel: 42235 / 6   Fax: (268) 46465
See display advert page 70

Phoenix Hotel
at Nhlangano
5th Street, Nhlangano
Tel: (268) 78488

Tambankulu Recreational Club
Tel: (268) 38111
Fax: (268) 38213
See display advert page 132

Phophonyane Lodge
at Piggs Peak
Tel: (268) 71319, 71429   Fax: (268) 71319
See display advert page 145

Tavern Hotel
in Mbabane
Tel: (+268) 42361/2 Fax: (+268) 40373
See display advert page 54

Protea Piggs Peak Hotel & Casino
Tel: (268) 71104/5   Fax: (268) 71382
Toll Free: 0800-11-9000
See display advert page 143

Timbali Caravan Park
Tel: (+268) 61156
See display advert page 73

Riverside Motel & Restaurant
Just before Big Bend going North
Tel: (268) 36012 Fax: (268) 36032
See display advert page 119

Yen Saan Hotel
Tel: (268) 61051, 61052
Fax: (268) 61051
See display advert page 81

CRAFT/TOURISM SHOPS

African Fantasy
Shop 11, The Mall, Mbabane
Tel: (+268) 40205, 61244
See display advert page 63

African Fantasy
at Mantenga Craft, Ezulwini
Tel: (+268) 61136 Fax: (+268) 61877
See display advert page 82

African Heritage
Swazi Plaza, Mbabane, Swaziland
Tel: (+268) 46083, 46765
Fax: (268) 46083

African Impressions
at Mantenga Craft
Telephone: (268) 61136

African Queen
at the Lugogo Sun Hotel
Ezulwini Valley
Tel: (+268) 61341

Baobab Batik
Tel/Fax: (+268) 83177
Nyanza, Malkerns Valley
See display advert page 101

Copperland of Swaziland
before Mantenga Craft
Telephone: (268) 61718, 42756

Coral Stephens
at Piggs Peak
Tel: (268) 71140 Fax: (268) 71178

Endlotane Studios
Showroom: Ngwenya
Tel: (+268) 45447/9 Fax: (+268) 45449
See display advert page 52

Fluidesign
at Mantenga Craft Centre
Tel: (268) 61136, 61431 (a/h)

Indingilizi Art Gallery
112, Johnston Street
Telephone 46213 Fax 46404
See display advert page 57

Likhaya Tapestries, Handicraft and Gifts
Ezulwini Valley
Tel: (+268) 61196

Likhaya Curios
Shop 25B, Swazi Plaza
Tel: (268) 46083

Living in Africa
At the Plaza, Mbabane
Tel: (+268) 46468 Fax: (+268) 43021
See display advert page 61

Little Silver Shop
at Mantenga Craft Centre
Tel: (+268) 61136 Fax: 61040
See display advert page 86

Mantenga Craft Centre
Ezulwini Valley
Tel: 61136, Fax: 61040
See display advert page 85

Ngwenya Glass
P.O. Box 45, Motshane
Tel (+268) 24053, 24151, 24142
See display advert page 50

Papaya
at Royal Swazi Sun Hotel
Ezulwini Valley
Tel: (+268) 61001

Parrott's
The Courtyard, in the Ezulwini Valley,
Kingdom of Swaziland
Tel (+268) 61269

Rosecraft
PO Box 192, Malkerns
Tel: (+268) 53915 Fax: (+268) 85033
See display advert page 116

CRAFT/TOURISM SHOPS

Sunny Bananas
at the New Mall, Mbabane
Tel: (268) 48605

Shiba Rugs
at Mantenga Craft Centre / Bethany Mission
Tel: (+268) 61136, 84821
See display advert page 102

Swazi Candles
P.O. Box 172, Malkerns
Tel (+268) 83219 Fax: (+268) 83135
See display advert page 101

Southern Country
at Mantenga Craft Centre
Tel: (268) 61136 Fax: (268) 61040

Swazi Flame
Swazi Plaza, Mbabane
Tel: (268) 40403

Swazi Crochet Centre
at Mantenga Craft Centre
PO Box 210, Ezulwini, Swaziland
Tel: (268) 61376 or 61136

Tekwane
at Protea Piggs Peak Hotel and Casino
Tel: (268) 71104
See display advert page 148

The Pine Corner
at Mantenga Craft Centre
Tel (268) 61136

Tishweshwe
Malkerns road, Malkerns
Tel: (+268) 83336 Fax: (+268) 43021
See display advert page 99

Tintsaba Craft
Highlands Inn, Piggs Peak
Tel: (268) 71260 Fax: (268) 71382
See display advert page 148

RESTAURANTS

Bend Inn Restaurant
at Big Bend
Tel: (+268) 36111 / 2 Fax: (+268) 36364
See display advert page 120

Calabash Continental Restaurant
Ezulwini Vallley
1km from Royal Swazi Sun
Tel: (+268) 61187
See display advert page 74

Creingos Restaurant
at Impala Arms Hotel
P.O. Box 34, Tshaneni
Tel: (268) 31244

Dining Hut (The)
at Phophonyane Lodge
Tel: (268) 71319, 71429 Fax: (268) 71319
See display advert page 145

Egumeni A La Carte Restaurant
Protea Piggs Peak Hotel
Tel: 71104/5 Fax: (+268) 71382
See display advert page 143

Fontana di Trevi
Shop No.5, The Hub, Manzini, Swaziland
P.O. Box 928, Manzini
Tel: (268) 53608 Fax: 52436

First Horse Restaurant
Ezulwini Valley
Tel: (268) 61137
See display advert page 81

Forresters Restaurant
Ezulwini Sun Hotel
Tel: (268) 61201, 61650
See display advert page 6

Foresters Arms Restaurant
at Foresters Arms Hotel
Tel: (268) 74177/74377
See display advert page 113

Friar Tuck Restaurant
at the Mountain Inn Hotel
Tel: (+268) 42781 Fax: (268) 45393
See display advert page 68

RESTAURANTS (cont'd)

Gigis Restaurant
at the Royal Swazi Sun Hotel
Tel: (+268) 61001
See display advert page 6

Maxims Restaurant
Johnston Street, Mbabane
Tel: (+268) 44640

Gil Vicente
Closed Mondays
Ilanga Centre Martin Street
Tel: (+268) 53874

Mediterranean Restaurant
Allister Miller Street, Mbabane
Tel: (+268) 43212
See display advert page 58

Hwa Li Restaurant
Ground floor Dhlan'ubeka Hse, Mbabane,
Tel: (268) 45986, 46534
See display advert page 67

Mocambique Restaurant
Tel: (+268) 52489/52586
See display advert page 106

Jubilee Restaurant
The Tavern Hotel
Tel: (+268) 42361/2
See display advert page 54

Nandos Chickenland
The Hub, Villiers Street, Manzini
Matsapha & Mbabane
Tel: (+268) 52330, 86573, 48580

Kentucky Fried Chicken
Mbabane, Manzini & Matsapha
Tel: (+268) 40433, 52402, 85997

New George Restaurant
Tel: (+268) 52061 - 4
Fax: (+268) 52061
See display advert page 107

L.M. Restaurant
Gilfillan Street, Mbabane
Tel: (+268) 43097
See display advert page 57

Pablo's Restaurant
Allister Miller Street, Mbabane.
Tel: (+268) 42406/42034
See display advert page 56

La Casserole
The Mall, Mbabane
Tel: (+268) 46426
See display advert page 64

Riverside Restaurant
Just before Big Bend going north
Tel: (268) 36012, Fax: (+268) 36032
See display advert page 119

Longhorn Restaurant
Swazi Plaza, Next to Stanbic Bank
Mbabane
Tel: (+268) 41729

Planters Restaurant
at the Royal Swazi Sun Hotel
Tel: (+268) 61001
See display advert page 6

Lubombo Lobster Restaurant
Just off the main road south of Big Bend
Tel/Fax (+268) 36308
See display advert page 120

Sailor Sam Restaurant
The Hub, Manzini
Tel: (+268) 53950

Marcos Trattoria
Allister Miller Street, Mbabane
Tel: (+268) 45029
See display advert page 58

Sir-Loin Steakhouse
at Happy Valley Motel, Ezulwini Valley
Telephone: 61061, 61199, 61898
See display advert page 87

RESTAURANTS (cont'd)

Simunye Country Club
Simunye
Telephone: (+268) 38133
See display advert page 136

Steers Fast Foods
The Mall, Mbabane
P.O. Box 305, Mbabane
Tel: (268) 43343

Siteki Restaurant
at Siteki Hotel
Telephone: (+268) 34126
See display advert page 139

Terrace Restaurant
at the Royal Swazi Sun Hotel, Ezulwini Valley
Tel: (+268) 61001 Fax: (+268) 61859
See display advert page 6

Snackies
Swazi Plaza, Mbabane
Telephone: (+268) 44405
(Closed 1.30 - 2.15 pm)

Yen Saan Chinese Restaurant
Ezulwini Valley
Tel: (+268) 61051/2 Fax: (+268) 61052
See display advert page 81

TRANSPORT

Avis Rent-a-Car
Tel: (+268) 86226, 86222, 86350, 38623 (a/h)
Fax: (+268) 86227, 84928
See display advert page 103

Scan Air Charters
at Matsapha Airport, Swaziland
Tel: (+268) 84474 a/h 52673 Fax: 86340
See display advert page 22

Imperial Hertz Car Rental
Tel: (+268) 84393/6, 84862 Fax: 84396
Mbabane: Tel: (+268) 41384 Fax: 40459
See display advert page 3

Scan Transportes Aéreos Lda
Mavalane Airport, Maputo
Direct line: Tel: 465592 Fax: 465525
See display advert page 22

Royal Swazi National Airways
Tel: (+268) 43486/7 Fax: (+268) 45984
Johannesburg (27) 11 331 9467/8
See display advert page Back Cover

Umhlanga Tours and Safaris
Tour desk - Royal Swazi Sun Hotel
Tel: (+268) 61001, 44522 Fax: (+268) 42485
See display advert page 33

TRAVEL AGENTS

Capital Travels
Swazi Plaza, Mbabane
Tel: 44143, 44257
Fax: 44257   Telex: 2188 WD

Sundown Travel
at Swazi Plaza, Mbabane
Tel: (+268) 40769 Fax: (+268) 44291
MAPUTO: Tel: (258) 1 423 740

Connections Travel Services
Swazi Plaza, Mbabane
Tel (+268) 42101, 42298, 41954
Fax: (+268) 46120 Telex: 2037 WD

The Travel Centre
Shop No.1, The Hub, Mhlakuvane Street
PO Box 1741, Manzini
Tel: (+268) 52983, 53955 Fax: 53829

Professional Travel Agent
at The New Mall, Mbabane
Tel: (+268) 41148

Ultra Travel
Manica Hse - Cnr Nkoseluhlaza & Martin Str.
Tel: (+268) 52237, 52872
Fax: (+268) 52137

AIN'T NO MOUNTAIN HIGH ENOUGH
DOCUMENTS, PARCELS, MOUNTAINS OR MOLEHILLS

WE KEEP YOUR PROMISES

No.7 Karlyn Centre, Coopers Lane, Mbabane
P.O. Box 83, Veni, Mbabane.
Kingdom of Swaziland.
Tel: (+268) 45829, 45830, 45831.
Fax: (+268) 45440 Telex: 3018 WD.

SWAZILAND JUMBO TOURIST GUIDE 5TH EDITION
Alphabetical List of Advertisers

CLIENT	PAGE NUMBER
AFRICAN FANTASY (THE MALL)	63
AFRICAN FANTASY (MANTENGA CRAFT)	82
AVIS RENT-A-CAR	103
BAOBAB BATIK	101
BARCLAYS BANK	38
BIG GAME PARKS	INSIDE FRONT COVER
CALABASH CONTINENTAL RESTAURANT	74
CITY INN	56
DHL	169
ENDLOTANE STUDIOS	52
ENGEN SWAZILAND	24
FIRST HORSE RESTAURANT	81
FORESTER'S ARMS HOTEL	113
FOTORAMA	37
HAPPY VALLEY	87
HAWANA PARK	152
HOTEL CARDOSO	159
HWA LI RESTAURANT	67
IMPERIAL CAR RENTAL	3
INDINGILIZI ART GALLERY	57
KING SOBHUZA MEMORIAL	97
L.M. RESTAURANT	57
LA CASSEROLE RESTAURANT	64
LIVING IN AFRICA	61
LITTLE SILVER SHOP	86
LUBOMBO LOBSTER RESTAURANT	120
LUCIANA	60
MACMILLAN BOLESWA	23
MALOLOTJA NATURE RESERVE	149
MANTENGA CRAFT	85
MANTENGA LODGE	86
MARCO'S TRATTORIA	58
MATATA SHOPPING CENTRE	118
MAXIPREST TYRES	41
MEIKLES MOUNT	114
MEDITERRANEAN RESTAURANT	58
MERIDIEN BIAO BANK	40
MGENULE MOTEL	72
MINISTRY OF TOURISM	66
MLAWULA NATURE RESERVE	135
MOCAMBIQUE HOTEL & RESTAURANT	106
MOCAMBIQUE PORTS & RAILWAYS	157
MOUNTAIN INN	68

CLIENT	PAGE NUMBER
NGWENYA GLASS	50
PHILANI PHARMACY	28
PHOPHONYANE LODGE	145
POLANA HOTEL	154
PROTEA PIGG'S PEAK HOTEL & CASINO	143
P.S. WOODWORK	138
RIVERSIDE MOTEL AND RESTAURANT	119
ROSECRAFT	116
ROYAL SWAZI NATIONAL AIRWAYS	BACK COVER
SARTOC AFRICA	108
SCAN TRANSPORTES AEREOS	22
SHELL OIL SWAZILAND	MAPS AT REAR
SHIBA RUGS	102
SIMUNYE COUNTRY CLUB	136
SITEGI HOTEL	139
SMOKEY MOUNTAIN VILLAGE	83
SPAR SUPERMARKETS (MALL & HUB)	62
STANBIC BANK	45
STANDARD CHARTERED BANK	17
SUN INTERNATIONAL	6
SWAZI CANDLES	101
SWAZI INN	70
SWAZI SPA HEALTH & BEAUTY STUDIO	75
SWAZILAND BOTTLING COMPANY	48
SWAZILAND DEVELOPMENT & SAVINGS BANK	94 & 95
SWAZILAND FRUIT CANNERS	100
SWAZILAND INSURANCE BROKERS	96
SWAZILAND INTERNATIONAL TRADE FAIR	105
SWAZILAND RAILWAY	INSIDE BACK COVER
SWAZILAND ROYAL INSURANCE CORPORATION	151
SWAZILAND SUGAR ASSOCIATION	128
TAMBANKULU RECREATIONAL CLUB	132
TEKWANE	148
THE NEW BEND INN HOTEL	120
THE NEW GEORGE HOTEL	107
THE TAVERN HOTEL	54
TIBIYO INSURANCE BROKERS	36
TIMBALI CARAVAN PARK	73
TINTSABA CRAFTS	148
TISHWESHWE	99
UMHLANGA TOURS & SAFARIS	33
WEBSTERS BOOKSHOP	8
YEN SAAN HOTEL	81

Shell welcomes you to...

SWAZILAND

TOURIST'S GUIDE MAP

Go Well Go Shell

SHELL IN THE FAST LANE

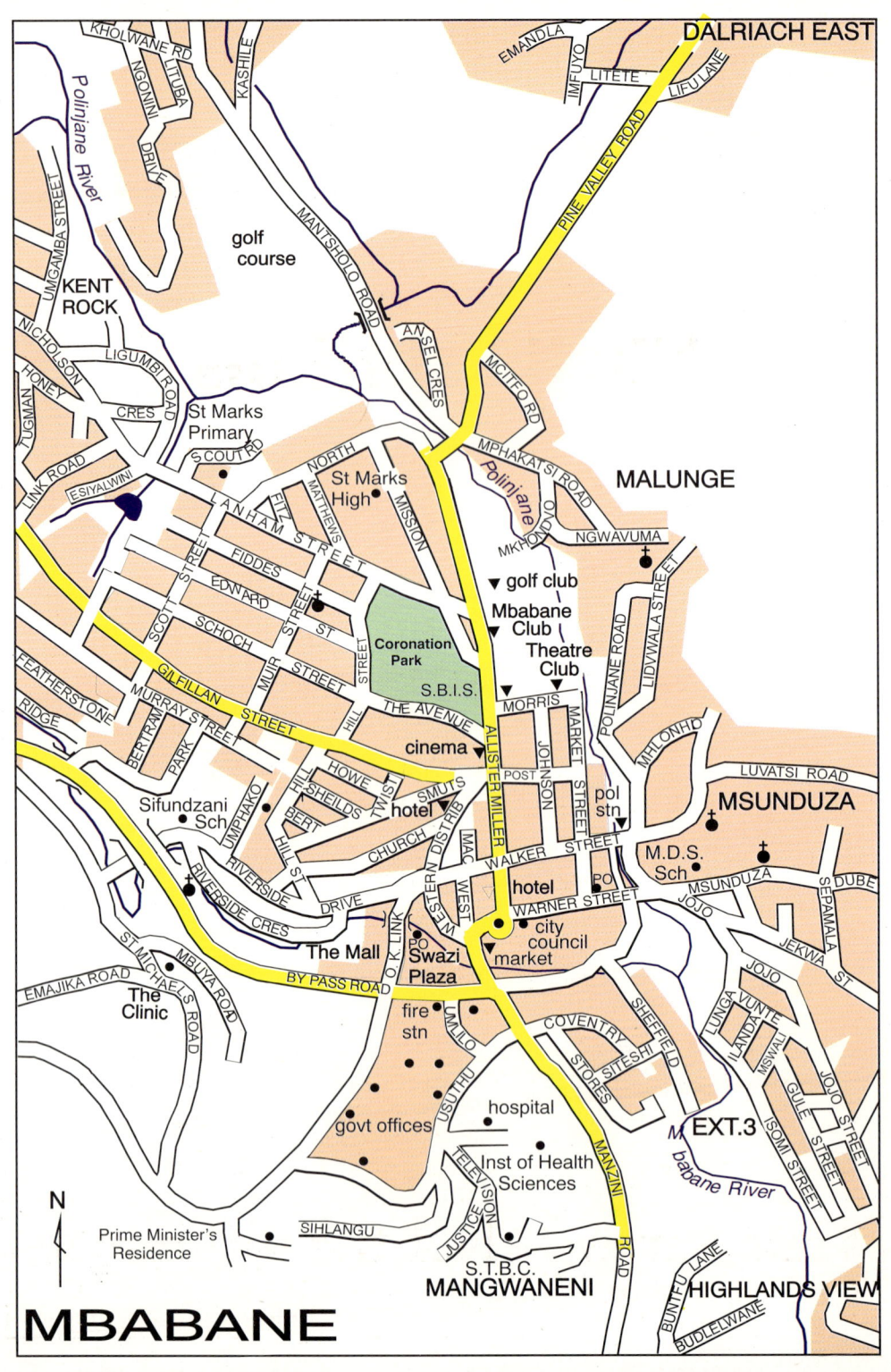

The biggest network in the country Shell stations

Your car will feel the difference.

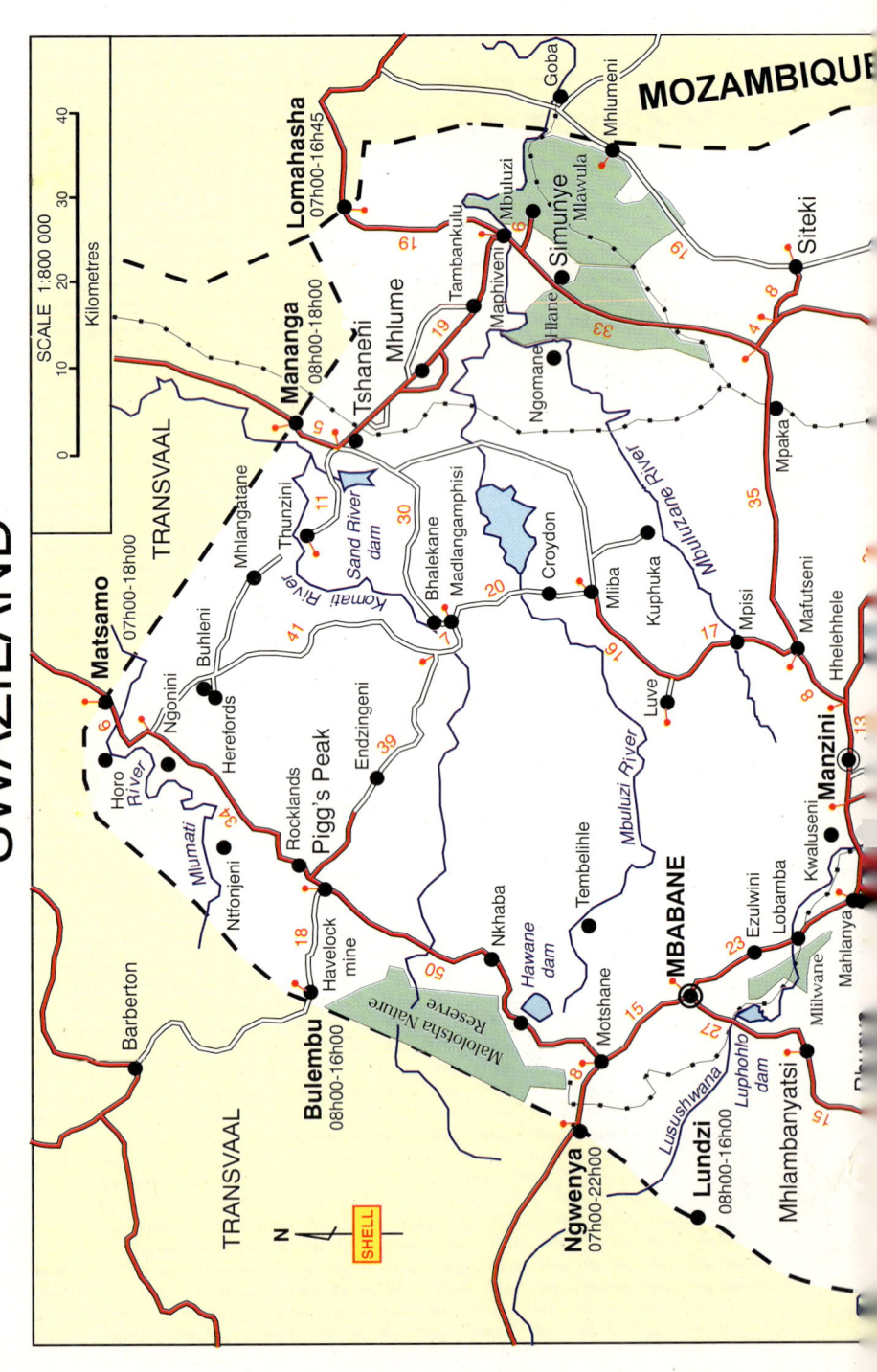

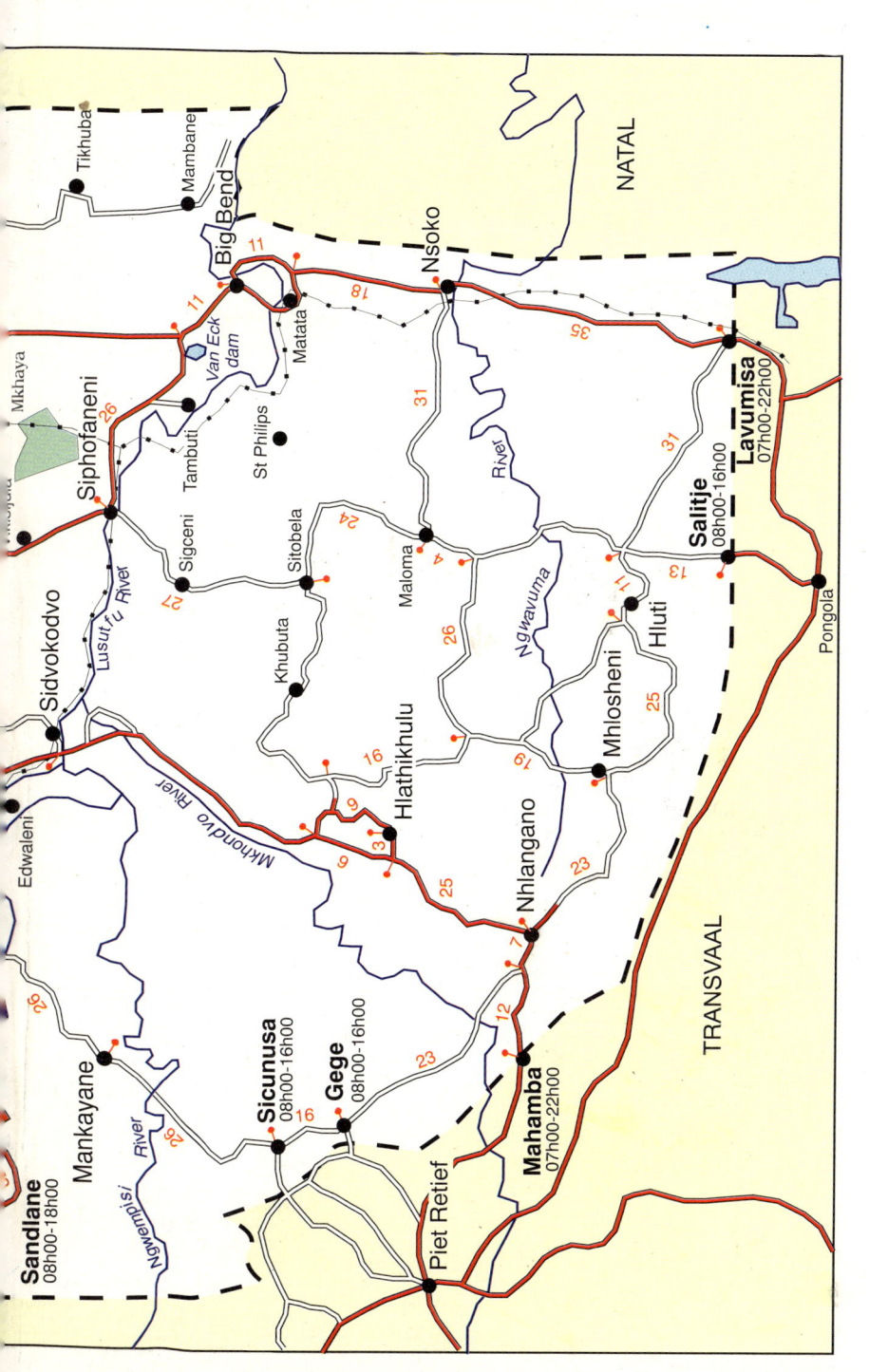

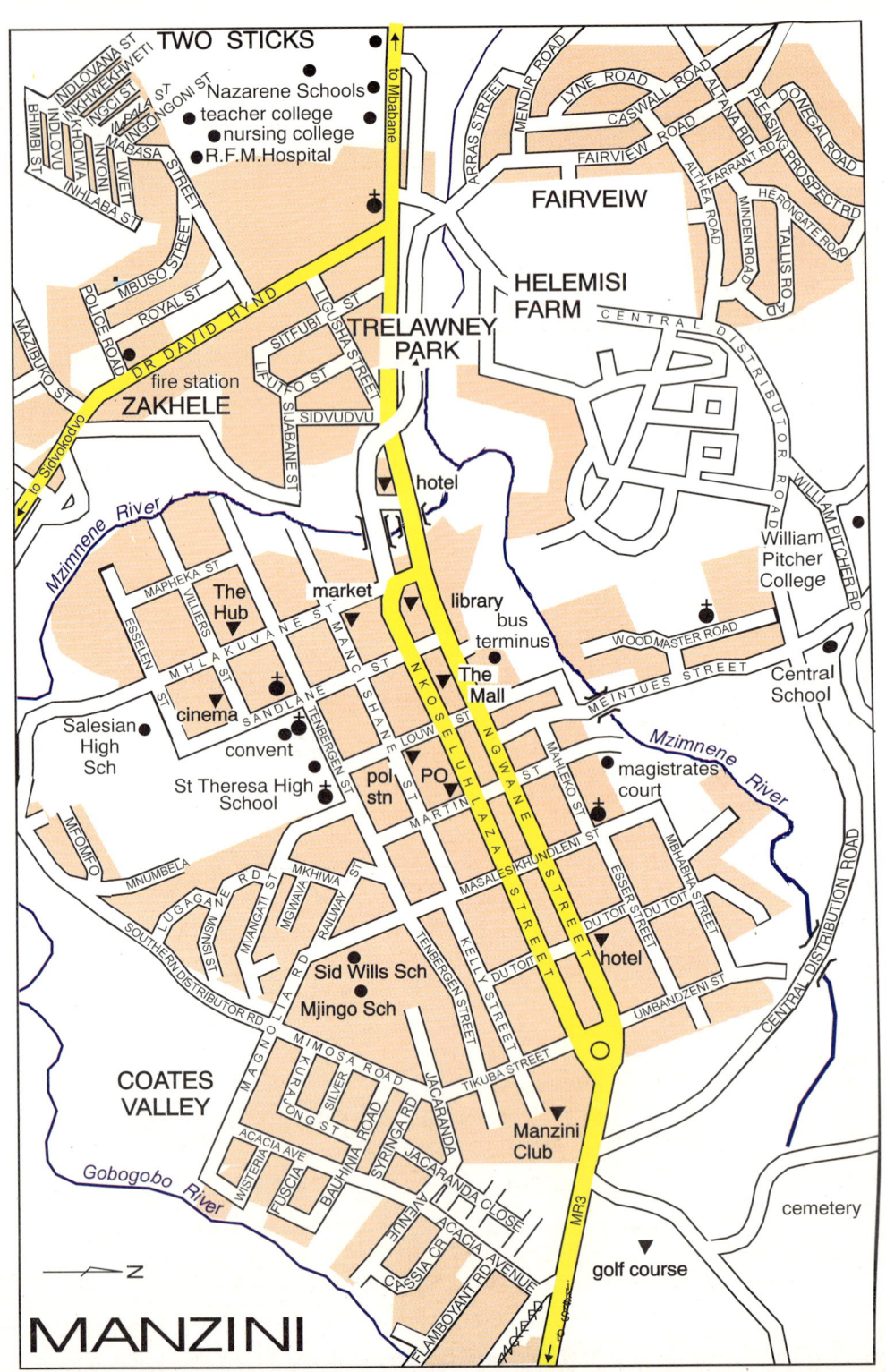